D1141493

MARY LAVIN
Quiet Rebel

By the same author

Liam O'Flaherty the Storyteller (London & New York 1976)

MARY LAVIN
Quiet Rebel

A Study of her Short Stories

A. A. Kelly

Wolfhound Press

17949

© 1980 A. A. Kelly
ISBN 0 905473 46 9
Published by
Wolfhound Press
98 Ardilaun Portmarnock Co. Dublin

Typesetting — Redsetter Ltd.
Printed in Great Britain by
REDWOOD BURN LIMITED
Trowbridge & Esher

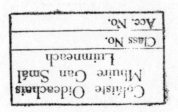

For my mother

Kathleen Russell Kelly

Acknowledgements

Permission to quote from Mary Lavin's work has been granted by the author herself, from whom I have received every possible help and encouragement.

I should also like to thank Brendan Kennelly, who first suggested the need for such a study; and Benedict Kiely and Seamus Deane both of whom advised on the first draft of the text.

A.A.K.

Contents

Acknowledgements   6

Frontispiece   8

Introduction   9

Chapter 1   The Social Hierarchy   19

Chapter 2   The Family and Intimate Relationships   47

Chapter 3   Religious Conventions   85

Chapter 4   Artistic Intentions   115

Chapter 5   The Significance of Textual Revisions   139

Conclusion   169

Notes on the Text   179

Bibliography   186

Appendix   190

Index   195

MARY LAVIN
(photograph by Mike Bunn)

Introduction

Mary Lavin was born in East Walpole, Massachusetts, on 11 June 1912, the only child of Irish parents. When she was nine her parents returned to Ireland at her mother's particular desire. Nora Lavin, who came from a large middle class family in Athenry, County Galway, had only settled in the United States after marriage and never liked it. Tom Lavin, twenty years his wife's senior, was from Roscommon and had emigrated to Boston in his youth. Mother and daughter returned to Athenry for a year, and then moved to Dublin when Tom rejoined them. In 1926 they moved again to Meath where Tom was appointed Manager of Bective House, owned by the American family for whom he had worked in East Walpole.

Mary must have had a peaceful and secure young life. She was educated in Loreto Convent, Dublin, and University College, Dublin, where she completed her Ph.D. thesis on Virginia Woolf, and wrote her first short story on the back of the typed copy. She then taught French at the Loreto Convent for two years. Her first story 'Miss Holland' and two poems were published in the *Dublin Magazine,* then edited by Seamus O'Sullivan, in 1939-40. Mary Lavin has written about fifteen other poems, all unpublished, all of which she says need re-writing. Lord Dunsany, a County Meath neighbour, also helped launch her work by introducing her to the editor of *Atlantic Monthly* and writing a preface to her first short story collection, *Tales from Bective Bridge*, for which she was awarded the James Tait Black Memorial prize in 1943.

When she was twenty-six Mary was taken by her father, now an old man, on a visit to the States, and it was after this that she started to write. Four years later she married a Dublin lawyer William Walsh, a friend from her University College days. They bought the Abbey Farm, Bective, when Tom Lavin died and divided their time between Meath and Dublin. Three daughters of this marriage were born in 1943, 1945 and 1952. A year after the birth of the third daughter William died, leaving Mary with three young children to support and the farm to run, while her mother continued to live with them. Mary was by this time an established writer with five volumes of short stories and two novels to her credit. For five years after her husband's death she says her production declined, and during the first two years she had no time to write at all. As her youngest child reached school age things became more manageable and the Guggenheim awards she obtained in 1959 and 1960 enabled her to branch out and regain artistic confidence, apart from giving her additional financial security. *The Great Wave* volume, which incorporates most of the work from this period, gained the Katherine Mansfield Prize.

In 1969 Mary Lavin married Michael MacDonald Scott, an Australian laicised Jesuit and old University College friend. In 1972-3 she was elected President of the Irish Academy of Letters. Today her time is still divided between Dublin and the Abbey Farm. Life is less complicated but she still finds it hard to work without being interrupted. Her early writing, she says, was often spoilt by haste. Much of it poured out and she wrote her second novel, *Mary O'Grady,* in a month, with many interruptions, during her father's final illness. She has since re-written and revised some of her earlier stories for republication in the British and American collected story editions.

Further details of Mary Lavin's life and attitudes are to be found in Zack Bowen's monograph,[1] and in her largely autobiographical short stories 'Lemonade', 'Happiness' and 'Tom'. She also identifies herself with the Vera Traske of 'Trastevere' and 'Villa Violetta' and with the Mary of 'In a Café'. Many stories, and the novel *The House in Clewe Street,* are set in 'Castle-rampart', the Athenry of her youth.[2]

Mary Lavin's ideas about writing are set forth in her ironically self-critical short story 'A Story with a pattern', written in 1939; in her Preface to *Selected Stories* (New York 1959); and in two interviews published in the *Sunday Press,* Dublin 1968, and *The Irish Times,* Dublin 1976. She has written no other criticism and dislikes taped interviews. In her Preface she says:

> Ever since I started to write a story in the middle of writing my Ph.D. thesis on Virginia Woolf — a thesis which I immediately abandoned — I have never, as far as I can recall, with the exception of a few words recently about my farm for a farming journal — I have never written a single paragraph that has not had its source in the imagination . . . . There was a time after I first started to write when I resented having so little time for stories, I used to think, with some bitterness, that if I were to cease writing altogether it would be months, even years, before anyone in my household would notice that this had happened — if they ever did! But now all that resent-

> ment has gone from me, and I believe that the things
> that took up my time, and even used up creative
> energy that might have gone into writing, have served
> me well. They imposed a selectivity that I might not
> otherwise have been strong enough to impose upon
> my often feverish, overfertile imagination. So if my
> life has set limits to my writing I am glad of it. I
> do not get a chance to write more stories than I
> ought; or put more into them than ought to be
> there.

She fears committing her critical opinions to paper
because 'only the stories seem to have finality and be
immutable'. She is a dedicated and painstaking artist
who now spends up to a year writing and re-writing
twenty or thirty drafts of one story, but her writing is
often done in 'snatches of time filched from other
duties', such as running the farm. Writing forms a
necessary foil to such practical activities. It is 'a way of
being' and 'only looking closer than normal into the
human heart', but 'the short story, shape as well as
matter, is determined by the writer's own character.
Because she believes in an intuitive way of writing she
admits that surprising compulsions may make a quite
unconscious appearance in her work. She believes that
'intuitive imagination can focus more directly upon
the object of its interest than memory or direct observation'. She expects her reader to be sensitive and
alert, to pick up 'devices of concentration, poetic
association, and above all implication'. The reader
should 'come forward to take the story into his own
mind and heart', for the story belongs to him just as
much as to its writer.

It is this reliance on instinct which makes Mary
Lavin's style so apparently casual. This does not — at
least not in her later work — imply carelessness, for she
is also a craftsman who goes back over her instinctive

response with a conscious desire to learn from and improve it. In *The Irish Times* interview she said about correcting earlier work:

> I feel very strongly about the ethics of altering early work. Seán Ó Faoláin has said that it is plagiarism for an older writer to alter the work of a younger person, the person that he once was. Well, I feel that if you have dedicated your life to the craft of the short story, as I have — and this is quite different from the craft of the novel — you really owe it to readers to correct mistakes that you see.

In the same interview about the genesis of the short story she said:

> . . . the real short story is possibly an idea, buried deep in the writer's consciousness, which he, miraculously at times, sees a chance of embodying in a story. I carry around a question in my mind, a question that teases and torments me for an answer, and then one day I think I see the answer in a person or an incident. But even then I don't rush and write it, it is only after I have encountered it a few times that I take the risk of inventing the story to house it in.

She considers the short story to be an intellectual medium, not only pure entertainment but also an enjoyable experience.

This study is based on the stories listed in the bibliography and excludes Mary Lavin's two novels. She has to date written about fifteen other stories besides these, most of which 'are not worth much'. Two of her stories, 'Cuckoo-Spit' and 'My Vocation' were recently televised by the BBC. Since 1960 she has had a contract with *The New Yorker,* still her main market. She writes irregularly but fast.

Augustine Martin said of Mary Lavin, 'she belongs to the thin front line of Irish short-story writers — to the company of O'Flaherty, O'Connor and Ó Faoláin',[3] but so far her work has received comparatively little critical attention. This is for several reasons: she does not set out to publicize herself, though in Ireland she is well known; her work is restrained in tone, the opposite of the current vogue in fiction; many of her stories will not appeal to the casual reader looking for a strong narrative line, who cannot be bothered with implication and innuendo; and she writes about neither politics nor nationalism. As Frank O'Connor said: 'Of the principal Irish writers of the period only Mary Lavin has come out of it unmarked . . . . Like Whitman's wild oak in Louisiana, she has stood a little apart from the rest of us, "uttering joyous leaves of dark green" . . .'[4]

V. S. Pritchett has pointed out that, 'there is commonly, in Irish writing, a double vision: the power to present the surface of life rapidly, but as a covering for something else . . . . Mary Lavin, who is describing the most ordinary people in provincial Ireland and without the colonial eye for bizarre effects, still displays the double vision and its unanswerable questions'.[5] Because of this 'double vision' much of the impulse behind Mary Lavin's work is ironic. She has never seen the world as a simple place. Her early, untitled, poem shows this:

> Christ if you wanted my shining soul
> That flashed its happy fins
> And splashed in the silent seas of sin,
> Then Christ, keenest fisherman
> on the Galilean shore,
> If you wanted to catch my shivering soul
> Why did you let down nets that were worn,
> Unravelled and floating light?
> I slid along the ribbony web

In and out
And when the nets slime-wet and black
Crawled over the prow of your boat again
Empty as nets that sway all day
In an empty sea
My sly soul waited
And swam aloft
To play at leaping the ripples
And showing its silver dapples
To the silently floating fishes
On the outer-side of the wave
The little silver minnows of the moon.

With its slightly over-pointed use of alliteration and internal rime this lyrical, moving poem contains many words expressing short time duration, 'flash', 'splash', 'ripple', 'dapple', or words of unstable and insecure implication, such as 'unravelled', 'ribbony', 'slime-wet'. There is an evanescent, fluid quality which voices uncertainty about the question posed. Because Mary Lavin has never found the answer she still writes.

We also see from this poem that the transcendent dimension is important to her. Her soul, called here 'shivering' and 'sly', would like to be caught up by an assurance of security, though paradoxically it would then cease its questive search and lose its ability for imaginative play.

In work of any literary value an important part of the meaning is implied not stated, and the writer has many ways at his disposal of conveying his implication, from the highly allusive and concentrated denseness of some poetry to the apparent simplicity of sparse, dramatized dialogue in which timing, pauses and silence all matter.

Mary Lavin's work is often concerned with delicate social nuance; the play of mind on mind; with the contrast of thought and speech in the same character;

the difference between the grand potential and the decrepit actual; the historic or philosophic ideal and the mundane enactment of it. She uses a carefully shaded pattern of meaning in which the strong reds and violets of dramatic tension appear but rarely.

Implication in her stories is often ironically expressed, showing the social concern but also the disappointment of her idealism. The ironic mode is used by a romantically inclined writer as a safeguard against disillusionment, to review himself and the contemporary situation at arm's length. Meaning stated ironically implies some degree of rejection by the author, the full intention of which may or may not get through to the reader, depending on his knowledge of the author's world, and to what extent he sympathizes with, or is prejudiced against, the author's views.

Mary Lavin does not want to pass on her vision of society by mirroring what she sees, or remembers, without simultaneously recording her personal opinion of this society's behaviour. The first three chapters of this study consider the body of her short stories through those areas of social concern against which her irony is most often directed. These are the social hierarchy, the family and intimate relationships, and religious conventions. Studying these three themes also throws emphasis on the particular milieu in which Mary Lavin's stories take place, and thus helps readers to pick up implications which might otherwise escape them.

But the idealism which leads Mary Lavin to wish to improve society by implying criticism of it is — as with all artists — mingled with her own search for identity and personal significance. We all reflect the society in which we live, and if we perceive what is false in our surroundings we may ourselves fear being subject to the same distortion. The fourth chapter consists of a more generalised consideration of Mary Lavin's intentions as an artist. How do her stories look more closely than normal into the human heart? How did her ability to do this develop with maturity? The narrative tones she uses act as one guide, for tone carries feeling. Feeling changes subtly as one character takes over from another, and the reader needs to be increasingly alert to pick up all nuance, especially those of the non-verbal response between communicating characters. Her use of place and description are also important in this context.

The fifth chapter goes on to consider the significance of the textual revisions Mary Lavin has made to her republished work, and what additional light these may throw on her artistic intentions and development.

V. S. Pritchett called Mary Lavin's stories 'mutinies of an observant mind, a record of unrepentant tumult where one did not know it could exist'; and so finally, against what is she in rebellion? And what specific contribution to the short story has she made?

Analysing a large body of short stories (the short story being a much less diffuse genre than the novel), the same story must sometimes be regarded from different points of view, and with each story we return to zero as far as treatment is concerned. The accretion of critical comprehension is therefore episodic rather than cumulative. The reader may, nevertheless, come to conclusions just as surely as he would after considering the more developed consecutive treatment from a smaller number of novels, and often more enjoyably, since he will be absorbing ideas through so many varied fabrications of reality.

1 The Social Hierarchy

In Mary Lavin's earlier work the reader is struck by how
conscious her characters are of their place in the social
hierarchy, whether they come from Dublin, small town
or rural Ireland, and how 'dated' therefore, in a social
sense, these stories have already become. The opening
passage of 'The Becker Wives' (1946) is an example:

> When Ernest, the third of the Beckers to marry,
> chose a girl with no more to recommend her than the
> normal attributes of health, respectability and certain
> superficial good looks, the other two — James and
> Henrietta — felt they could at last ignore Theobald
> and his nonsense. Theobald had been a bit young to
> proffer advice to them, but Ernest had had the full
> benefit of their youngest brother's counsel and
> warnings. Yet Ernest had gone his own way too:
> Julia, the new bride, was no more remarkable than
> James's wife Charlotte. Both had had to earn their
> living while in the single state, and neither had
> brought anything into the family by way of dowry
> beyond the small amount they had put aside in a
> savings bank during the period of their engagements,

engagements that in both cases had been long enough for the Beckers to ascertain all particulars that could possibly be expected to have a bearing on their suitability for marriage and child-bearing.

It is taken for granted that Ernest has 'chosen a girl'; that the 'normal attributes' for a bride should be good health, respectability and looks; that both brides worked while single but now, it is implied, will do so no longer; and that certain moral standards are necessary. It is delicately suggested that the girls are chaste, amenable to their future husbands' wishes and sufficiently competent domestically. A modern reader at once knows that the scene is set in the earlier part of this century.

'The Becker Wives' is one of Mary Lavin's group of longer stories, or novellas. The length of the story gives her scope to develop the characters within it; the four Becker brothers, James, Ernest, Samuel and Theobald, their wives Charlotte, Julia, Honoria and Flora and the Becker sister, Henrietta, and her husband Robert.

The Beckers are the *nouveaux riches* offspring of Bartholomew, a successful corn merchant with firm principles whose wife, big, soft Anna's dowry was simply 'Content' with a capital 'C'. 'It was inevitable, of course, that the more money Anna inspired her husband to amass, the more her beauty became smothered in the luxury with which he surrounded her', and the children of this marriage have, also inevitably, different ideas, especially Theobald, educated as a lawyer, who is a social climber. Theobald thinks it was all right for his father to marry the daughter of his head salesman but 'it was another thing altogether for his sons, whom he had established securely on the road towards success, to turn around and marry wives who were no better than their mother'.

We are given many vignettes illustrating the

materialistic values and social pretensions of the Beckers. Their genteel names, none of which are shortened, also reflect their pretentiousness. Henrietta, Julia and Charlotte become 'fat, heavy and furred', yet, like Anna, exude, in spite of the money lavished on them, 'an air of ordinariness and mediocrity' which makes Theobald squirm. Theobald tells his brother Samuel: 'I hope you'll have some aspiration towards a better social level', but is disgusted when Samuel marries 'this mediocre Croker person' Honoria, the daughter of another rich merchant. It is not more money the Beckers need, they have too much already, but 'distinction'. Theobald, in search of this ill-defined quality, brings the ethereal Flora into the vulgar Becker household.

Flora is not only physically small but 'doesn't eat as much as a bird'. Henrietta has enough imagination to describe Flora before they meet as: ' . . . a little creature, volatile as a lark, a summer warbler, a creature so light and airy that it hardly rested on the ground at all'. Flora's ethereality, however, extends to the opposite extreme of the heavy, earthy grossness of the Beckers. She is too frail to accept reality. She appears 'entirely unconscious of her person' but in fact everything she does is carefully calculated for effect. Far from lacking self-awareness, she is neurotically self-conscious. She spends her time posing and performing like a small bird caught in the Becker cage.

Underneath the ironic banter, throughout this story runs a serious vein of social commentary. The conventions and preoccupations of class and creed happen to be those current among social upstarts in Dublin in the 1920s and early 1930s, and a full consideration of them all would take many pages. It is evident that Mary Lavin finds such people ridiculous, even repulsive. She has drawn too exaggerated a picture of their foibles for us to believe anything else.

Much of the social snobbery of this period was based on the ideals of Victorian and Edwardian gentility with which Irish society, particularly in Dublin, was permeated. V. S. Pritchett in his *Dublin: a portrait* remarks of his first visit there in the 1920s, 'one was taken back thirty to fifty years into the domestic scenes of a Victorian novel, into unbelievable gentilities and snobberies . . . at the same time thrown forward into the first conflict of colonialism. This contradiction continued until post-war.'[1] Of his recent visit to Dublin before producing the book he added: 'The Victorian age which finally disappeared in England in the 1930's has lingered on in Dublin. One has to reckon on the time lag created by the Irish Sea . . . . The gentility, the accent of refinement and the snobbery, very pronounced in the 20's, still exist . . . . Each person is conscious of his family connections, especially as related to Irish history. In this there is a similarity with all colonial societies; and, of course, every person (and even a lot of places) are thought of as Protestant or Catholic.' This was written over ten years ago, we must remember.

The term 'colonial' society and the continued consciousness of religious adherence are both Pritchett's personal interpretations. Many would argue that it is more probably taken for granted that a person is a catholic, and with the younger generation nowadays (except in Ulster) far less attention is paid to the question of religion. The 'colonial' aspect of Ireland, if one can disregard the pejorative tinge to this term, has now merged into a national image, and young Irishmen and women of today have a far stronger sense of national identity than those of Mary Lavin's generation, who reached adulthood around 1930. Because Mary Lavin's parents came from small towns, and looked towards the United States and not Britain, her own inherited social prejudices were not attached to the 'colonial' aspect of Dublin society, which would therefore appear all the more ridiculous to her.

'The Becker Wives' is, moreover, much more than a piece of irony against social snobbery, for with the arrival of Flora the story takes on greater psychological and emotional depth as it becomes obvious that Theobald, who prides himself on having more sensibility and acuity than the rest of the family, is quite incapable of understanding his fey wife. Flora constantly seeks 'to escape from the tedium and boredom of the present'. Her life is based on pretence and elusion, and her mind eventually becomes deranged.[2]

The distinction between external and internal reality is what 'The Becker Wives' is about, with the Beckers representing those whose realities are external and Flora one whose realities are internal. In the story excessive attachment to the one leads to crass materialism, to the other, to madness. Of all the Beckers it is Samuel who from time to time makes timid attempts to introduce some balance between the two realities:

> Samuel had enjoyed his dinner. He was also enjoying the walk home. The streets late at night had an air of unreality that appealed to him. Like limelight the moon shone greenly down making the lighted windows of the houses appear artificial, as if they were squares of celluloid, illuminated only for the sake of illusion. He hoped Theobald wouldn't insist on dragging him back to reality. But he might have known better.

The extreme sensitivity of Flora is also creativity gone to seed. She enters so deeply into the minds of others that her impersonations invade her own personality and in her liking for Samuel, as the most imaginative of the Becker men, she ends by entering a permanent elusion whereby she becomes Samuel's pregnant wife, Honoria.

Such is the attention paid to the exterior details of manner, foible and appearance that the careless reader may stop there, believing the story to be about the ridiculous aims of the *nouveaux riches* and nothing else. He will be mistaken. Mary Lavin often writes at two levels of significance, one exterior and obvious, one hidden and implied. Both levels are to be found in 'The Becker Wives'.

In 'Miss Holland', Mary Lavin's first published story, the same expression of the dichotomy between two senses of reality, using the social frame to set the scene, is shown in quite a different way.

Miss Holland is a maiden lady who has come down in the world. In the first paragraph we are told that she had never heard before what a mattress is stuffed with. The stuffing of a mattress seems indecent and private, like the inside of the body, or the privacies of the bedroom. She is deliberately evasive and vague. 'She always wanted to avoid knowing why she did things because it was so much nicer not to know.' She has lived in a genteel cocoon spun in the shadow of her father. There is a part of Miss Holland which has never grown up, so that when she first arrives in the boarding house dining-room she is reminded of school. Old fashioned in her fastidiousness and her Victorian determination to shut her mind to unpleasantness, never to be bored or discouraged, the implications of the social distinction she feels between herself and the other boarders is ironically conveyed, all the more effectively because Miss Holland tries so hard not to be a snob. She knows little material things are much less important than deep values and sincere feelings. She wants to be accepted and liked, but the hypersensitivity she has developed in her past seclusion, with its rigid social conditioning, sets up an unbearable tension of uncertainty within her. She has to reconstruct her own frame of reference in a different environment, among different people. The mass of detail contained in her new circumstances impinges on the forefront of her consciousness like multiple darts of irritation (the ugly mantelpiece in her room; the other boarders' casual manners and careless speech; their acceptance of the second best) destroying her inner peace which has been based on withdrawal. Forced out of her vagueness she tells herself not to be stupid, these young people are more alive than she ever was. 'They don't notice the ugliness of their rooms. They ignore small points of difference between tailor-made and ready-made clothes. They transcend these things. They speak of life with courage and vigour.' But she fears they are as critical of her as she is of them. She thinks they find her old-fashioned, whereas in fact they are too preoccupied to take much notice of her. She has no confidence in herself: 'I can only talk about books and about pictures and about music. I cannot talk about the real problems of life.' So gradually her personality becomes paralysed.

Trying to accept the standards and attitudes of the other boarders she becomes more and more obsessed by her failure to conform. She is like a woman from another planet who, though she understands the conversation around her, cannot communicate at the non-verbal level, and is not used to men who walk through doors in front of women, speak coarsely and roar with laughter at the wrong moment. Her standards are swept away and she finds nothing to put in their place.

Finally Miss Holland, so well brought up that her feelings remain under strict control, tells herself: 'I must define their ugliness, their commonness, their bad taste.' But all she can name are warts, perspiration stains, false teeth. She does not realise that it is none of these things but the collapse of her own self-image which makes her so unhappy.

There is double irony in this story but with admirable impartiality the author's censoriousness falls alike on

the sense of reality held by both parties. On the boarders, not because of their brash manners and grease-stained clothes, but because they represent a new generation full of zest and vitality but with distressing signs of superficiality, aware of the world in a broad sense, but inconsiderate and tending to expediency rather than moral integrity. It is not manners and social etiquette being criticised here, but insensitivity and shallow feelings. This is shown in the tone of Mr Moriarty's account of how he shot the damned cat in the backside. The boarders' laughter floods Miss Holland's mind, described in terms of blood-like colours as ugly red fading to putty brown. 'She felt that they were the faces of people who did not exist, people in a nightmare, from whom she must get away immediately for ever and ever.' Her world, her sense of what is real, is not theirs. She is too sensitive — they are not sensitive enough. Each aspect is equally unbalanced. Has cultured gentility of the Victorian era degenerated with mass education? This is only so if the gentility Miss Holland typifies also implies consideration of others, but — as Mary Lavin also shows — Miss Holland's world was considerate only inside its own exclusivity, holding itself apart from, and by implication superior to, the common herd.

In both 'The Becker Wives' and 'Miss Holland' the ironic treatment of the social hierarchy, different illustrations of snobbery and class consciousness, mask criticism of profound issues far more enduring than the particular social ephemeralities involved. These issues are the surprising compulsions behind Mary Lavin's intuitive method of creating which mark the artist rather than the journeyman.

Zack Bowen says of Mary Lavin: 'Her vision of reality is harsh and closely circumscribed by an acute awareness of social class, and society's sanctions and rules. This is more than merely the theme of some of her stories; it is the donnée of her plots as well as the context of motive and constraint which conditions the behaviour of most of her characters.' He finds that along with personal problems Lavin's characters often have to deal with poverty and, even more, with an inflexible social order and caste system, so well defined and predictable that Lavin can often treat a town collectively as a character. 'The rules are Victorian, mean and all-pervasive. There is no mercy for those who violate them, attempt to evade them, or have pretensions above their station.'[3] This is a strong statement. It stops at what I have called the exterior and obvious level of significance in Mary Lavin's stories, but merits further investigation.

It is true that the class consciousness of the earlier twentieth-century society was more marked than that of today. There was still a servant class and, in Ireland, the remains of the Anglo-Irish 'ascendancy'. Of the four stories in *The Becker Wives* volume, 'The Joy-Ride' and 'Magenta' are about servants enjoying themselves in their master/mistress's absence. 'The Joy-Ride' is ironic in tone throughout, and contains an amusing description of the overseer's qualifications for being a gentleman. The story is about two butlers who take an old pony trap, a hunter and three bottles of curacao from the wine-cellar and go out for a day while the overseer is absent. During their jaunt the Manse catches fire. Though this story is a little contrived for modern tastes it has good narrative tension and character revela- tion and a heart-warming description of County Meath scenery. 'Magenta' relates how two maids, left as care- takers in a large house, put on airs of 'noblesse oblige' and patronise the poor village girl, Magenta, whom they engage to scrub the stone passage. The story reveals the pathetic pretensions of all three characters, trying in different ways to achieve status in the eyes of the world. Other stories about servants, or the servant/master relationship, are 'Sunday brings Sunday', 'Posy', 'Scylla and Charybdis', 'An Akoulina of the Irish Midlands', 'A Single Lady' and 'A Cup of Tea', while a paid companion is the principal character in 'The Small Bequest' and a housekeeper in 'The Mock Auction'.

Mary Lavin's acute awareness of social class is, in all these stories, a faithful reportage of attitudes commonly held at the time when events in the story take place; thus she brings servants into stories when they would normally have been found in middle and lower middle class households which, in Ireland, lasted well into the fifties. As all her earlier work is about people living in stable communities, whether urban or rural, the 'caste' system forms part of the normal social scene. This scene becomes less class conscious, reflecting the evolution of society, in her later work. Her social framework is always apt and accurate, but in almost all her work it clothes, or colours, the core of the story which lies underneath.

In 'A Single Lady' the story opens:

> Apart from anything else he wasn't that kind of man; the reverse indeed; distant; cool in his manner. And as for his manner towards the servants, in her mother's time at least he used to treat them as if they were made of wood; as if they had no feelings whatever. Latterly, of course, things had changed so much that they both had only the one wretched creature for all the drudgery of the great barrack of a house, there had been times when she herself had felt it necessary to be familiar.

The servant/master relationship provides the social colour of this story, but its major theme is more enduring than social ephemerality. The unmarried daughter of forty is 'educated and intellectual'; a dowdy spinster who has not spent one night away from home for twelve years. A more forceful version of Miss

Holland, Isabel — like Miss Holland — has, since her
mother's death, been close to her father, so she is
jealous when a relationship develops between him and
the servant Annie Bowles: 'As for the creature's room,
in spite of the fact that she knew it was her duty to do
so, she had never once gone into it. She knew so well
what it would be like: smelly and close, the windows
never opened, and the bedclothes bundled about like
rags. A servant indeed! Too good a word for her!'

Yet this servant had entranced her old father and
Isabel is powerless to stop it. The relationship between
the old man and the girl may be based on love, or
merely on lust — but this neither we nor Isabel can
judge, and the objective narrator gives no clue. The
difference between Isabel and her father is illustrated
by the description of Isabel's shoes, narrow, pointed
and old-fashioned, and her father's polished, dapper
ones, overhung by socks and underclothes. The story
centres round the inability of this middle-aged virgin to
understand the intimacy of two people whom she thinks
the strictures of social convention should keep apart.

Isabel's externally acquired intellectual wisdom is
contrasted with the internal 'secret wisdom' of the
loins and/or heart possessed by Annie which in the end
Isabel admits she cannot grasp either physically or
emotionally.

The second time the story was published in Volume
I of *The Stories of Mary Lavin* the final four lines, in
which the ironic message is baldly stated, were wisely
omitted.

'Lilacs', one of Mary Lavin's earliest stories, is about
respectability built on dung. Again the irony is obvious,
but this is redeemed by the human interest awakened
by the characters as the story progresses. Phelim and
Rose Molloy live off the profits of dung-dealing and
educate their two proper daughters Kate and Stacy.
Rose remembers that Phelim had said: 'There's a lot in

the way you think about things', and he compares the
dung flashing by under the horses' feet to pale gold
rings. Rose (or Ros as she more prosaically becomes in
old age) reminisces beside her husband's coffin about
their past life together. For her, love overcame the smell
of dung. The imaginary perfume of the lilac which Stacy
would like to grow on the site of the dunghill, mingles
in this story with the smells of lilies and guttered out
candles round the dead body of Phelim, but as Kate
says of dung: 'It's not the smell of it, but the way
people look at us when they hear what we deal in.'

As in many of Mary Lavin's stories the sisters
represent two different types of women, the idealistic
impractical Stacy and the hardhearted, ambitious Kate
— the Mary/Martha female types who so often confront
each other in Mary Lavin's work and who also each
symbolise preponderant leanings towards the external
or internal world. Stacy has headaches from the dung
and dreams of a huge lilac sprouting through the floor
boards. She faints at Ros's laying-out and again at the
cemetery. Kate determines that the dunghill will remain
until 'I have a fine fat dowry out of it', and she
eventually marries, leaving Stacy with dung as her sole
means of support, and no lilacs. One cannot live off all
smells, only productive ones. Dung is waste or dead
matter, but also a fertiliser.

The importance of respectability also occurs in 'The
Will', in which Kate, the eldest sister, tells Lally, the
sister cut out of her mother's will because she married
beneath her, that she has lowered herself by keeping
lodgers. The brother Matthew agrees, and Kate adds:
'It's not a nice thing for my children to feel that their
first cousins are going to free schools in the city and
mixing with the lowest of the low, and running messages
for your dirty lodgers. And as if that isn't bad enough, I
suppose you'll be putting them behind the counter in
some greengrocer's, one of these days.' Those with pre-

tensions to respectability did not do such things then.

In this painful story the selfishness and snobbery of Kate, Nonny and Matthew are explicitly conveyed as they rake their down-at-heel sister with their tongues and, 'All of them, even the maid servant who was clearing away the tray, were agreed that it was bad enough for people to know she was going back the very night that her mother was lowered into the clay, without adding to the scandal by giving people a chance to say that her brother, Matthew, wouldn't drive her to the train in his car, and it pouring rain'. But Lally runs off on foot.

What 'they will say' is paramount; outward appearances are what matter.

With Lally, however, the inner reality is the true one. She married for love. She still loves her mother because for her: 'Life was just the same in the town, in the city, and in the twisty countryside. Life was the same in the darkness and the light. It was the same for the spinster and for the draggled mother of a family. You were yourself always, no matter where you went or what you did. You didn't change . . . . There was only one thing that could change you, and that was death. And no one knew what that change would be like'. She runs to the priest and promises money for three masses, to be scraped out of her lodgers' rents, in spite of the fact that her mother, who died leaving Lally in want, had bequeathed £300 for masses to be said for her own soul. Lally, thinking of the torments of Purgatory, could not care less about what people think. This story also shows that imbalance in exterior/interior priorities leads to abnormal behaviour for the mother puts the care of her own soul before the earthly welfare of her daughter.

Frank O'Connor said of Mary Lavin: 'She has the novelist's preoccupation with logic, the logic of Time past and Time future, not so much the real short-story teller's obsession with Time present — the height from which past and present are presumed to be equally visible . . .' and thought her most important work would be written in the form of the 'nouvelle'. He predicted that these longer stores would be 'more expansive, more allusive, more calligraphic' than those written earlier.

Since O'Connor wrote these lines Mary Lavin has written another half-dozen novellas and revised both 'The Becker Wives' and 'A Happy Death' for republication. The revised 'A Happy Death' fulfills O'Connor's prediction and well illustrates Lavin's clever use of time; indeed it is the way she wields the shuttle of time back and forth in this story which creates the dramatic impact. The implications of giving principal place to outward appearances are here stretched to melodramatic limits, and the focus is again on respectability.

The plot line, though still taking second place to the narration of mental states, as in most of Lavin's work, is unusually strong, and there is an exact and graphic description of each scene so that actuality and the setting of the story is held in dramatic tension with the interior development of Ella's thoughts and sensations, there often being incongruous contrast between the two.

We first see the household through the eyes of Nonny, aged eleven, youngest of the three daughters, who calls upstairs to her mother in the dark lodging house. The lodgers are all female and her father, the only male in the place, is simply referred to as 'he'. The other two daughters are Dolly, who works in a chemical factory, and Mary with a crippled back, apprenticed to a dressmaker. Mary is weak and sensitive like her father Robert, of whose youth she has built up an idealistic picture. Dolly is practical and, like her mother, easily exasperated.

When the story opens the father, with 'less authority

in the house than any of them', is coughing and moaning in the kitchen. Gradually we learn why his wife treats him so callously and how she has constructed a barrier of self-hate through which self-pity often seeps. At first the reader, no more than Ella's daughters, does not quite understand what is the trouble between the couple, 'their mother's complaints, and their father's justification of her, were expressed in such similar words they missed the distinguishing emotion that underlay the words'. It is the tracing of this emotion which makes this story so intricate, chiefly because the outward expression of it is at variance with what, by the end of the story, is finally revealed.

Mary Lavin develops the past social situation by flashback and Ella's reminiscence. Ella, daughter of a well-to-do shopkeeper, eloped with Robert when they were aged nineteen and twenty; they have been married twenty years. During this time Robert's delicate physique, which originally appealed so much to Ella, has deteriorated rapidly and now, the house full of lodgers, he sleeps in the damp back kitchen.

Ella has developed defensive mechanisms to cope with the aspects of reality she cannot face. She has become embittered and neurotic: 'the thought of his loyalty to their outworn romance did not soften her, and she told herself that it was easy for him to talk about those days, down at the Library, where there was no one to see how the romance had turned out, where there was no one to see the drudge he had made her, and the way she had gone to pieces. She'd like to tell people about the old days, too, but she had to hold her tongue, for who'd believe now that she was ever young, or that she ever had soft hands and fine skin'.

We learn that Ella has always been obsessed by the external and though Robert's interest in poetry had at first entertained her she soon grew impatient with it: 'The day she gathered up all the old books and threw them into the fire he said nothing for a minute, and then he said she had done right'. Robert tells her then: 'A man can't expect to walk with his face turned up to the sky without losing his foothold on the ground. You must keep your eyes on the ground'.

Though the ground, upon which both now keep their eyes, becomes more and more squalid Ella persists in pinning her hopes to appearances — brilliantine, new collars and shoes; but she pays little attention to Robert's inner man, physical or emotional. Finally he is reduced in status from librarian to janitor, where his coughing will not disturb the readers. The lodgers' money Ella now regards as the sole support of the family and she sneers at the small sum Robert brings home each week. His manhood erodes under her gibes but 'when he got fits of coughing, or an attack of the cramping pains across his chest her own viewpoint only narrowed down the more'.

Ella's obsession with the trappings of respectability is just as unbalanced as Flora's retreat into the personality of another in 'The Becker Wives'. Ella tells Robert: 'You're keeping me back. People won't take rooms everywhere and anywhere, and when they hear my husband is a janitor they think the place isn't class enough for them. And when they see you going in and out, in your dirty old clothes, coughing and spitting, that turns them more against the place; whereas if you were to give up that job and stay at home and wear your good suits, and put on clean collars it would make the place look respectable'.

Robert's health finally gives way. Ella is at first appeased by this for now she will no longer be humiliated by her husband's work status. He can become a gentleman again. The gentleman she had originally married.

But Robert's illness is incurable. The final part of the story takes place round his deathbed in hospital. In this graphic section we once more see Ella obsessed by the respectable things a patient should be brought, regardless of expense. We see the realistic reactions of the daughters, ignored by Ella. Mary's view is: 'Mother doesn't feel any remorse. If she did she would be upset. She would probably break her heart. But I don't think she is aware of the way their lives were wasted away in bitterness. I think it just seems like a bad spell they got into and that it will pass away and they will come out again into a bright happy time like they used to have long ago. She doesn't blame herself at all. She thinks they were both the victims of misfortune'.

Ella could not be accused of hypocrisy, though the implication is there. She is, rather, obsessed by social conformity. In hospital she behaves exactly the way a distraught wife should. She now calls her husband frequently by name: 'Robert! Robert! Is there nothing I can do for you? Why don't you know me? It's Ellie. It's your own Ellie! Ellie who'd do anything in the world for you!' Sadly enough she is sincere in this, for Ella has passed beyond any real capacity for love. The external is the only reality she understands and even an expression of the spiritual has to take outward form. She is now deluded into thinking that Robert will recover to become her tame gentleman. It is only when the nun offers an alternative outlet, 'the grace of a happy death', that she turns her attention to the outward signs of the last sacrament. Now, instead of bags of oranges 'there was an accumulation of cruci-fixes and blessed candles, holy water and medals, all of which by turns she pressed against his lips and fore-head and his hands in the hope that they would bring him back from the hopeless silence into which he had sunk', for the words of contrition must be said.

The deliberate exaggeration of Ella's obsessiveness stretches verisimilitude to breaking point, only held in abeyance by the dramatic tension of this scene, contrasted as it is with the deathbed conversion of the atheist at the other end of the ward. The scene verges on the melodramatic but there is enough truth in it to give the reader pause. The sincerity shown by delirious Robert, living in the past, ironically seems more sane than Ella's reactions to the present, and this maintains the reader's respectful attention as it becomes evident that Robert, whose point of view we have not heard until now, has remained pure in heart and full of love for his wife. The rapturous way he dies, without saying the Act of Contrition, shows happiness, but the story ends 'it was utterly incomprehensible to Ella that God had not heard her prayers, and had not vouchsafed to her husband the grace of a happy death'.

This complex story illustrates once again the dichotomy which may exist between external and internal states of reality, apparent in the incompatible attitudes of this couple; the tragic gulf which may open between ideals, or spiritual realities, and the inadequate and mistaken human enactment of them. Mary Lavin has used, in O'Connor's expression, the 'logic of time' to form this story and impose some order on the illogical chaos of emotions and memories.

Love, loneliness and death all enter 'A Happy Death' which starts from an obsession with social pretension based on the finite and ends with an intimation of immortality based on the infinite, making it one of Lavin's best attempts at the novella form.

More often, however, the ironic element of a story outweighs its tragic content as in 'The Small Bequest', in which snobbery about breeding is ridiculed. This story tells how Miss Blodgett, paid companion to rich old Miss Tate of ancient lineage, is finally deprived of the money bequeathed her because she is designated ambiguously in the will as 'my fond niece Emma', whereas in fact she is no blood relation. The theme of this story is the revelation of Miss Blodgett's insensitivity, shown by her stupidity at presuming to call her employer 'Aunt Adelaide', thus implying that she is on a par with the superior Tates who have nine generations behind them.

In the re-written version of this story, among a multitude of other small changes, the observant first person narrator takes her holiday in the west of Ireland instead of the south of England. The story could, however, be set in either country. The stress on breeding is English, or Anglo-Irish, and all the characters have English names. Beneath the apparent tranquillity in the peaceful garden scenes seethes the frustration of Miss Tate, who reacts waspishly whenever Miss Blodgett addresses her as 'Aunt Adelaide', and whose real feelings, though they remain hidden to Miss Blodgett, are adroitly suggested by the narrator. Mary Lavin uses the description of outward detail to reveal states of feeling and awareness. There is Miss Tate with a patrician aquiline nose, dressed in pure silk; buxom Miss Blodgett with thick ankles, in artificial silk; and Hetty 'only a servant' who wears Miss Tate's cast-off clothes and is as astute as her mistress. After Miss Tate's death the prudent Hetty is in a better financial position than Miss Blodgett, who has always patronised Hetty as her social inferior. Hetty's niece now calls Miss Blodgett 'Emma', while Miss Blodgett calls her 'Miss Hynes'. Here, as in 'A Single Lady', we see the instability and change inherent in social structures, and there is again implied criticism of the incompetent sheltered woman who is too stupid, or refined, to stand on her own feet.

Mary Lavin's 1951 volume of stories, *A Single Lady*, shows the slow erosion of the older and more class conscious way of life, often pointed out by a narrator who may, or may not, have a personal role in the story. This occurs in 'A Gentle Soul', another story about two contrasting sisters, Agatha and Rose, in which the narrator Rose is the gentler of the two. The action of this story is retrospective, set on a small farm in the

days of the narrator's youth when she first falls in love
with her father's labourer Jamey Morrow. Speaking of
their neighbours she says:

> Perhaps old Lanigan was not as proud as our father,
> and did not set such a high standard for his women-
> folk, allowing them to walk to Mass sometimes rather
> than take out the trap, particularly if the day was
> wet, and taking less heed of their appearance in the
> house too . . . . But whatever might have been old
> Lanigan's laxity in these respects, he and Father saw
> eye to eye when it came to estimating the difference
> between themselves and the labouring class.

Rose and Jamey never get beyond a few stolen words
together. Rose stifles her love — she lives a vivid interior
life but allows external circumstances to control her;
Agatha, the materialistic sister, reflects their father's
views. In support of his social status their father is
willing to force Rose to commit perjury. Rose betrays
her loved one's memory because her love is throttled by
fear.

Early in this bitter little story Rose looks back at
those days of her youth: 'Who, for instance, could have
thought when this country got its freedom and they
began to build ugly little concrete houses with hideous
red-tiled roofs for the labourers and farm workers,
that a day would come when they would be fitter for
human habitation than our farmhouses that were such
a source of pride to us'. Here lies the clue to the social
frustration. They had so little that they clung
tenaciously to whatever small, imagined superiority they
possessed.

In 'Posy' the young girl has the courage to slough off
her small town social caste by escaping to Dublin.
The narrator is a well-dressed young visitor who arrives
seeking information, and is directed to the shopkeeper

Daniel. Most of the story is related, again in retrospect, through Daniel's reminiscences. Daniel has two older sisters, Kate and Hannah, who keep him tied to their apron strings. Daniel has never left his birthplace and is now a timid sixty-year-old bachelor. Posy, the nickname of their servant girl of long ago, is a similar character to Onny Soraghan in *The House in Clewe Street*. The sisters have great respect for the professional class and when the elegantly dressed young man turns up Daniel takes him for a solicitor from Dublin and shows him a consequent amount of respect. Daniel explains to the young man that he never thought of marrying Posy, of whom he had been very fond, because his sisters had said: 'how would you like to have people throwing it in the face of your children that their mother was a chit of a servant girl from the back lanes of the town?' Daniel adds: 'And I came to understand it, of course, after a while. I'm surprised that you don't understand it, sir; a man of your position'. But by the end of the story it is obvious that the smart visitor is none other than Posy's son.[5]

Mary Lavin is always acutely aware of the social framework in which her characters move. For small shopkeepers and farmers of her youth, society was very hierarchic, to the modern mind unpleasantly so. This framework then provided a solid social structure against which the surface of life could be painted in, and we have to look below this surface to find the deeper reality of the better stories. She sets many of her early stories in her own youth — or gives them retrospective action — reverting to a world that had already largely passed when she wrote, but whose values were more precisely definable than the shifting ones of the immediate present.

In 'What's Wrong with Aubretia' (also published as 'The Villas' in 1959), Mary Lavin shows us a contemporary character wishing, but not quite being able,

to break away from her inherited social inhibitions. The
opening lines set the scene: 'They were standing inside
the big gates at the entrance to the avenue; the gates
that were one more anomaly now as the villas invaded
the small fields to either side of the drive'. The story is
about the conflicting feelings and attitudes of Vera
aged thirty-four, whose family once owned all the land
on which the villas are built, and Alan aged thirty who
lives in one of them.

The story starts by outlining the exacerbation
existing between the pair based on their different social
heritages, and then continues to unfold other facets of
their relationship in which feeling and prejudice contra-
dict one another.

'It's a question of class, I suppose?' asks Alan, dis-
cussing their different opinion of the villas. Vera is
quick to deny this; like Miss Holland she wants to
believe the difference is based on taste, but Alan is not
convinced. 'Taste is the new euphemism for class',
he says, thus pinpointing the new unstable measurement
which is taking the place of the older hierarchy. He continues: 'There's no such thing as class nowadays; not in
places like this anyway, not in any form'. Class has
become vague, like a fog, 'you get lost in it'. Both these
characters are, in fact, a little lost and though each
denies the existence of social class each is proscribed by
inherited attitudes based on class. Alan is nervous with
Vera's father, and feels the big house is 'browbeating'
him. He is intelligent, well educated and determined, a
hard-headed realist not given to introspection, and to
him houses had, until then, been just places to eat and
sleep in. He has 'no time for what is called love, and
absolutely none for love at first sight'. Vera is equally
intelligent and well educated but also romantic, aestheti-
cally aware, divided between the old values she has un-
consciously absorbed in her youth, and the new ones
she knows, logically, should be put in their place. Alan

is on his way up and out, perhaps to a job abroad where he can create his sense of identity undisturbed, whereas Vera is anchored by her attachment to her father. Alan's relationship with Vera has unsettled him and caused him to question his prerogatives. He says: 'It was you who opened my eyes'. He had taken it for granted 'that you'd have me, if circumstances were otherwise'. It hurts his pride that these circumstances stand in his way and he is not prepared to adjust his life to them. They are an ill-assorted pair living in a changing social climate.

Alan might return to Ireland when he has created his social identity outside the country, as so many have since done. Vera can only hold on to what she knows, that big brass knob in the middle of the old door, and unhappily take refuge in dreams, unless her father dies soon enough to release her. The indirect tone and vague ending of this story express the social dilemma.

In one of Mary Lavin's more recently written novellas, 'The Mock Auction', the protagonist, Miss Lomas, is followed over an unspecified period of years lasting a generation. She moves out of the old world and into the new, in which a fragment of Crown Derby china is used to stop up a mousehole.

Miss Lomas is another dependent woman. She is 'grafted' to Brook Farm, owned by the two Anglo-Irish Garrett brothers who live in Garrettstown. 'She was one with it and it was one with her'. Like Miss Blodgett in 'The Small Bequest', over the years she builds up her status as the farm housekeeper, does not bother about a salary as such, queens it over the dealers, vets and land inspectors, for whom she has hearty meals prepared, and never steps on a cowpat. Outward respectability and status is highly important to her.

The foil to Miss Lomas is Christy, weedy, orphaned son of a younger Garrett sister who married beneath her into an unsuitable catholic family. He has been reared on the farm by his uncles' charity.

The story is about the gradual deterioration of Miss Lomas' status as first one and then the other Garrett brother dies suddenly, and the farm becomes the property of the wastrel Christy who has neither the money nor the energy to maintain it. Mr Parr, the solicitor, handles the legal details, is patronised by Miss Lomas and called simply 'Parr'. Miss Lomas, like Miss Blodgett, lacks intelligence. When the mock auction is suggested it was not 'until she had consulted her cookery book and pondered what she felt to be analogous instances in mock-creams and mock-turtle that Miss Lomas got any grasp at all of the plan'.

'The Mock Auction' is at one level directed against the pretensions of Miss Lomas, but she is also the vehicle through which the reader observes social change. Her illusions of personal grandeur are stripped away. At the end of the story, when she and Christy confront one another in the decaying house, her Victorian gentility about money is ridiculed as Christy throws her a dirty ten shilling note: 'That might hold your bones together until they come and take you away'. Miss Lomas, left alone in the house for the first time goes and makes the inevitable cup of tea, thinking to herself 'it was so long since she had handled money it seemed of no more use than a toffee-paper. Disdaining it, she looked away. Had she not always been above money? Indeed, it seemed to her at that moment that there was really no need for it. If only people would behave properly and it could be done without, she felt sure. Had she not proved this?' And here the narrator adds 'But to whom? Only to herself!'

Like Flora in 'The Becker Wives' and Robert in 'A Happy Death', Miss Lomas increasingly takes refuge by escaping from reality. Her sortie to Garrettstown, during which she appears in her outdated clothes on the road where motor-cars and not traps now flash by, makes her withdrawn state very obvious, but does nothing to awake in her a sense of her own predicament. She is fixed in the habits of the past and maintains a core of dignity based on memory of what once was, amid the physical wreck of the house, and in spite of her penury. This dignity and what in the end is revealed as a genuine attachment for Brook Farm, are the two things which make Miss Lomas pathetic, rather than merely objectionable.

Mr Parr, the small town lawyer, says that in the old days Brook Farm 'would have been far too grand for the likes of me', but in the end he thinks of occupying the farm with his widowed sister and her children. His pimply nephew, who calls Miss Lomas an old bag, will be one of the new tenants.

Mary Lavin's farming knowledge emerges in this story, and also her love of the land which endures beyond the social ups and downs of ephemeral human beings who all end up buried beneath it.

Looking back now over this group of stories what are the didactic implications of Mary Lavin's ironic use of class-consciousness? What are her own intentions? The stories are set in Dublin, in small towns or in the country. Characters range from members of the Anglo-Irish ascendancy to the poor Dublin family struggling to maintain vestiges of respectability; from the aristocratic pretensions of Miss Tate to those like Posy, who have no pretensions at all. In all the stories opposing pairs, or sets, of characters are contrasted, and it is through their direct reactions to each other, or sometimes to the narrator's comment on their mutual reactions, that the difference between them is brought out.

In some stories such as 'The Becker Wives' and 'A Happy Death' the contrast is carried to tragic proportions in the story's plot, but brought back by the narrator to a reasonable and unemotional objectivity at the very end of the story. In 'A Happy Death' the narrator is finally less preoccupied by the tragic degeneration of Robert's character and physique than by his wife's insistence on externals. In 'The Becker Wives' our attention is withdrawn from Flora's tragic insanity and focused on the supposedly eminently sane Beckers. The ironic implication is, in both cases, re-stressed at the end of the story and is in each case left for the reader to interpret himself. It is only if we feel more sympathy for Ella than for Robert, for the Beckers rather than for Flora, that we may question this implication. In 'A Happy Death' the revelation of Ella as a character is carried far beyond that of any one character in 'The Becker Wives', so that we feel pity for her as well as for Robert, and the drama of their personal crisis outweighs its ironic implications, right up to the narrator's final paragraph. But in 'The Becker Wives' the collective reaction of the Beckers, from which Theobald and then Samuel's reactions are dis-tinguished, never carries the revelation of character very far. The Beckers remain a group, the 'them' and 'them-selves' expressed in the last few lines.

In both these stories the imaginative life is stifled, or perverted, by the harsh and materialistic view of reality held by the dominant character, or group of characters.

In all the stories mentioned the characters' social awareness finds an outlet in social pretensions of one kind or another, depending on the strata of society they come from, or aspire to. These characters may be practical realists, like the Beckers, Miss Tate, Ella, Agatha Darker; those whose feelings take second place to practical necessity like Kate Conroy in 'The Will', Daniel in 'Posy'; or those for whom social awareness entails some bewilderment and a desperate clinging to their social role, as if this is the only reality they under-stand. Their awareness can be circumscribed by stupidity, social seclusion, or both, as with Miss

Holland, Miss Blodgett and Miss Lomas. In the later
story, 'What's Wrong with Aubretia?', we see Vera
trying to escape from a predetermined role in life, for
she is neither stupid nor socially secluded. In all the
earlier stories, pretensions, whether based on class,
family, social role or superior education resulting in
better taste or more intellectual knowledge, are
ridiculed.

The impractical, dreamy characters are less worldly:
Flora carries her artistic tastes too far into the realms
of fantasy; Robert allows his love of poetry to be
nullified; Stacy dreams and smells lilacs but has no
practical sense at all. Many of the characters who
represent the other world, that internal world or inner
reality of dream, instinct, fantasy and meditation, lack
will power, the ability to order their thoughts, the
courage to act, physical resistance, or all of these things.
They may be shown as a sloppy old man sitting with the
maid in the kitchen, or as a drunken wastrel like Christy
— only two escape, Posy and Lally. Our knowledge of
Posy's later life is limited to her putative son's remark
'As a matter of fact I have cause to be grateful to her
myself', while Lally, though not hamstrung by
materialism, cannot formulate her thoughts clearly.

It may be inferred that Mary Lavin intends to show
the perpetual and necessary dichotomy between the
outward and inward senses of reality; the ability to act
and to dream; the tension between reason and instinct;
and the extreme difficulty of resolving this dichotomy
in a balanced way without developing an excessive
concern with materialistic detail on the one hand, or
escaping into negative illusionary or static states on the
other. Her attention to snobberies of class and social
pretension implies that as an accurate social commen-
tator she finds twentieth-century society preoccupied
with the material and the actual.

2 The Family and Intimate Relationships

The majority of Mary Lavin's stories take place between intimates or within the family and it is through her treatment of family relationships that the world of her stories is revealed. Some sixty percent of her stories are related from the female point of view, that is through a female character or by an obviously female narrator who may, or may not, be the author, and reading Mary Lavin one is conscious, more often than not, that a woman has written the story. Why is this?

We have already considered her treatment of the help-lessly dependent female character and those who extract a spurious feeling of superiority from their social status to mask the narrow emptiness of their lives. She also shows men leading dull lives and though some, such as Manny Ryan of 'At Sallygap', dream of escaping, others — like Danny in 'Posy' — do not.

Mary Lavin's feminine point of view emerges not only through her choice of domestic subject matter, but also through her delicate but restrained attention to small detail and the intuitive response. The fact that she so often shows the social conditioning of the feminine state, means that she is herself very conscious of it, and

though attitudes between the sexes evolve in her later
stories with a modern setting, restraint — not to be
confused with prudishness — remains. Emotional relationships between characters are largely implied, often
expressed by feeling rather than words, or else trivial
conversation is used to indicate communication passing
beneath it at a non-verbal level. Such wordless feelings
in Lavin stories are conveyed by deceptively simple
prose in which the meaning resides in understatement,
tone, or ironic hint.

Social conditioning must naturally affect the attitude
of the female writer, though she may — as Edna O'Brien
has done — rebel against it. Her femaleness must also
play a part in her subconscious artistic response upon
which the metaphoric is often based, and in her conscious comparisons.[1] A woman writer who has given
birth would never compare noise to the cries associated
with labour pains, 'full of Sound and Fury, signifying
nothing', as Liam O'Flaherty once did.

Mary Lavin's writing is circumscribed by her particular circumstances. Wisely, she has concentrated as
an artist on what she knows and understands best. She
is better describing the female than the male point of
view, and more at home in the domestic story, only
making an occasional foray into a different genre in
stories such as 'The Green Grave and the Black Grave'
and 'The Great Wave'. Woman's role, intimate human
relationships and particularly the radiant presence of
love, evidently intrigue her. Even the dreariest life may
be redeemed by love and her irony on this subject is
directed against the obstacles or barriers already existing
in society, or erected by human beings against the
admission or recognition of love as paramount.

In small town or rural Ireland of the earlier twentieth
century, about which Mary Lavin so often writes,
opportunities for women were limited. The young girl
shown in 'Sunday brings Sunday' is expected to be

'nice good biddable'. She lies in bed, 'impatiently whittling away at the hickory stick of her childhood. She had no heed for the hours ahead that she must have known vaguely would be filled with the noises of dirty wash sousing and grey slop spilling, coal hods clattering and the noiseless run of wet wood splinters into the soft wet palms of her hands'. It is a grand opportunity for her, when she thankfully leaves school, to become maidservant to the doctor. The narrow experience and incredible naivety of this girl must at one time have been typical, and still exist among simple people in many parts of the world.

Narrated mostly through the girl Mona's dreamy and inconsequential interior monologue, her thoughts ironically express her social situation. When she asks Jimmy about sex, which neither understands, the sweat appears as large drops of fear on his face and he reminds her of a sheep. 'She thought of the great white faces of her father's sheep when they were penned up waiting their turn for the shearing. The eyes of the sheep used to be dark and full of dread in their white faces and that was the way Jimmy looked in the dark hayrick, as if something dreadful was going to happen and he didn't know rightly what it was'.[2] This young pair are so heavily conditioned by the narrow circumstances of their upbringing that they have hardly yet emerged from the innocent dreamworld of childhood. The girl conceives in ignorance, and her fears will cause love to be stillborn.

'Sunday brings Sunday' could be contrasted with 'The Young Girls' from the same volume, *The Long Ago*. This story is about the smart twenty-first birthday party of the well-to-do Ena, to which the adolescent sister Emily has invited three girl friends. The lives of these young girls, from a much higher social bracket than Mona, are already geared to the admiration of men. 'Men don't like girls that look too young', and 'blushing is attractive' are two romantic illusions. It is a major calamity when they think Dolly has damaged her reputation by going down to the river with a young man whom she has only met at the dance for the first time. The girls decide, 'Anyway you can't judge men by our standards. They are not chaste by nature the way we are'. A more informed but still heavily conditioned innocence appears here: 'Sitting along the rim of the cold porcelain bath in their thin silk dresses, they felt exceptionally chaste indeed, and staring down at the tiles on the floor it seemed that even the music that only faintly reached them was nevertheless a travesty of their vague virginal antagonism to everything — oh, but everything — in the world'.

These lines, conveying a wordless and intuitive state of mind, contain the kernel of the story. The girls are chaste not by choice but because of their tender years; but their state of chastity will continue after marriage has broken its physical barrier for it is rather· a withdrawal of the mind, vaguely based now on inexperience, tinged with fear; a state to be admired as future chaste wives and mothers. The perfect chastity of the Virgin Mary, conceived without sin, hovers unexpressed as an ideal in the background. Remembrance of the social conditioning received by young Irish girls, catholic first, Irish second, female third, is a necessary adjunct to the full understanding of unexpressed feeling in these characters. It is the same antagonistic feeling, a desire to remain unbroached, unspotted, whole, contained, and at the same time on another and perhaps superior plane from the majority, which enters into stories such as 'The Nun's Mother' and the recently written 'Eterna'.

In 'The Long Ago' the emotional implications of woman's married state are contrasted with spinsterhood. This story is set in Athenry in the days of Mary Lavin's youth. It is clear from the start that Dolly and Ella, who are married, pity their unmarried girlhood friend Hallie.

Hallie had once loved Dominie, who married Blossom and died young. Blossom has remarried and Hallie has taken to tending Dominie's grave. She has bought a plot of land beside him even though Blossom will eventually be buried beside her first husband. Spinsterhood is socially inferior:

> After all, it wasn't fair to regard Hallie as an old maid. She had been the prettiest of the three of them, and she had a nicer disposition. If Dominie Sinnot had not been a worthless weakling, Hallie would have been married before either her or Ella. If it came to that, Hallie could have married someone else, even after Dominie married Blossom, if she hadn't remained so absurdly wrapped up in him.

Hallie lives a lonely life. She has 'kept intact through the years the web of her romance' with Dominie so that after first Dolly's and then Ella's husband dies, she considers herself in the same bereaved category. But the self-centred single state of Hallie can never be the same as that of the memory-enriched widows Dolly and Ella. To them the past 'was a misty place, in which it was nice to let their minds wander, but which they knew they could never re-enter, whereas Hallie had never left it'. Hallie omits to recognise that marriage is not just romance or security, but also a physical state containing duties, responsibilities and shared experience which may even include love. As Dolly expresses it: 'a widow was not the same as a woman who had never had a man in the house at all!' The exclamation mark is ironic in the context, for it indicates some of Dolly's repressed and more intimate thoughts.

The odours and intimacy of family life, and the possession of a husband are more explicitly revealed in 'The Inspector's Wife', in which Dolly compares her married life with Tom, the cattle inspector, to the easy

single state of Miss Anna Falconner, the rich society girl.
Dolly, envious of Anna's social position, comforts herself by thinking that she can still make Tom whistle.
Happy marriage to a fine-looking man with thick hair
and a strong body is of prime importance to a woman
in spite of any drudgery it may involve. Dolly's life,
with five young children, is one of hard physical work
and sacrifice. Love is not mentioned yet the emotional
pleasure she gets from her husband and family are a
compensation:

> Now and again when she was turning back the sheets
> to air them in the mornings the hot smell of the night
> rose up out of the blankets and she buried her face in
> them and breathed it in with a kind of fervour. There
> was a queer pleasure, too, in smelling the children's
> soiled clothes and Tom's used shirts . . . . Those warm
> odours were a sort of symbol of marriage; an intimate
> secret, penetrating symbol of something Dolly never
> thought about directly.

A wife's determination to put up with things is
differently expressed in 'The Haymaking', in which
Chris Glebe, the well-off farmer with three hundred
acres, thinks he will pick his wife like a filly in the ring
by measuring her pelvic depth with his eyes. In fact he
becomes fascinated by Fanny the townbred school
teacher when she is sitting down playing the piano.
Fanny marries Chris because she is bored with teaching
and farmlife sounds romantic. Once their honeymoon is
over Chris shows her little affection, only rudeness and
sarcasm. He regards her as a possession, useful if she is
productive. He is the masterful husband with all the
rights and Fanny decides she must, like a good wife,
adapt herself. Chris tries to break her spirit. By the end
of the story all romance has left their marriage. Fanny
no longer notices the beauty of the land. She is moulded

to her husband's image and has become a mere echo of his mind, obsessed with the fertility of crops and yield. Love has never entered their arid relationship at all.

A more extended consideration of love in the family framework is illustrated by a group of stories about the shopkeeping Grimes family, Matthew the father, Tom, Bedelia, Alice and Liddy, who live in Castlerampart, Mary Lavin's fictional name for Athenry. 'An Old Boot' first reveals the family circumstances, though Alice and Liddy have already appeared in 'A Visit to the Cemetery'. The other Grimes stories are 'Frail Vessel', 'The Little Prince' and 'Loving Memory'.

In 'An Old Boot' we meet the family a month after the mother's death. The father has retreated into senility and spends all day locked in the upstairs parlour; Bedelia has taken charge of the shop. Business is bad, the brother Tom feckless, and the two young sisters think only of marriage. Bedelia tells herself: 'It was all very well for them to snap their fingers at the business, but the shop was all the husband that she'd be likely to get, and she wasn't going to let it slip out of her grasp'. But she soon marries Daniel, the shop assistant, 'a man of the meek and humble kind that would never push himself forward'. Daniel is her fate; he knows how to run the shop. Marriage for practical purposes, and getting married at all costs, are foremost in Bedelia's mind.[3]

It is ironic when at the beginning of the next story, 'Frail Vessel', Bedelia, already married to Daniel, criticises her young sister Liddy for romantically marrying Alphonsus O'Brien. Bedelia is jealous of Liddy. Her real feelings emerge once in the story when, 'two rare, very rare, and angry tears' are squeezed out of her pale eyes' — tears of self-pity. The narrative tone of this story makes the implications clear and the dichotomy between the practical realist and the dreamy idealist, a feature of so many stories, is shown in these sisters. Bedelia represses more than she will admit, when Liddy recounts how she has imagined her feet touching those of Alphonsus — 'after we were married I mean!' — Bedelia puts out her two hands: ' "Keep back from me", she shouted. "Hurt indeed. Disgusted would be more like it! Such talk from a young girl!" '

Bedelia's shallow feelings for her sister, based on self-interest, are revealed in all their mockery when Liddy says that she too is pregnant. In spite of her difficult circumstances, by the end of the story Liddy has 'a radiance and glory about her that Bedelia could not but perceive'.[4]

In Liddy love triumphs. From her emanates purity of feeling, and in the second half of the story, where the narrative is unfolded partly by the objective narrator and partly through the ironic revelations of Bedelia's interior monologue, there are intimations of the precedence of true feeling, the unselfish love of Liddy, over the practical schemings and hypocritical connivance of Bedelia. Liddy, in spite of her inferior social and material status, retains her moral integrity. She possesses the same indestructible love as Lally has in 'The Will'.

Love related to the married state occurs much less frequently in Mary Lavin's earlier work than marriage as an escape, as social security, or as a status symbol in which love, if it plays any part at all, soon wilts and dies.

The fourth Grimes story, a rather rambling novella called 'The Little Prince', shows a more equivocal Bedelia. The time span of this story stretches over forty years, the point of view being sometimes Bedelia's and sometimes Daniel's. The title refers to Tom, the only Grimes brother, who as a child was treated royally but grew up to be a weak, aimless man. Bedelia easily persuades him to emigrate but years pass and he never writes or returns to claim his accumulated share of the shop's profits. In the end Bedelia and Daniel set out for

New York to try and establish the identity of an old tramp named Tom Grimes, sick in hospital and perhaps their brother. Some softening in Bedelia's feelings occur as they near the New York hospital:

> For the first time since she was a child, there was no connivance in Bedelia's heart. All considerations of money had faded from her mind. It was as if an angel of light had come and sat down beside her in the dark cab, illuminating everything with a blinding radiance. Daniel, who looked at her covertly, saw a great change in her face, but he did not know what to say or do. As for the light that shone for her, so blindingly beautiful, he was as unregarding of it as of the light of day. For in it, like millions of other simple men and women, unwittingly he had lived out all his life.

This radiance is the memory of love, aroused by reflection about her brother as a child. Yet when she comes before the corpse of the old man: 'She looked again into the dead man's face. But if it was her brother, something had sundered them, something had severed the bonds of blood, and she knew him not'.

She never discovers whether or not this is Tom. Neither does it matter whether he is, in the flesh, if he is not in the spirit. The ties of love have been cut, and the biblical overtone of 'she knew him not' expresses the betrayal of her trust. The purblind Bedelia stumbles eagerly back into the cab hoping to regain the radiant feelings she has previously experienced, but her heart: 'was too old and cracked a vessel to hold any emotion at all, however, precious, however small a drop. There was no angel sitting in the cab. It was stuffy and close, and smelled strongly of feet'. We are brought back with this suggestive anti-climax, to something earthy Bedelia can understand.

The last Grimes story, 'Loving Memory', reverts to the Grimes parents called here Matthias (not Matthew) and Alicia, so that it is set in the time of Mary Lavin's parents and one suspects it is her mother's family she has used as a basis. There are deliberate non-sequiturs in events between one Grimes tale and another. For instance, in 'The Little Prince', the child Bedelia is expecting in 'Frail Vessel' is never mentioned, and in 'Loving Memory' Alice, not Bedelia, is the eldest of the four children.

The older Mary Lavin becomes the more intricate and elusive is her portrayal of fleeting human emotions, and the more baffling the shifts of tone and argument when she uses the ironic voice. In 'Loving Memory' there is a great deal of teasing which can only be disentangled by comparing the presented view of things with the author's unspoken evaluation, and the reader needs to be perceptive to guess what this is. No small quotations from this story can therefore convey its total effect.

The story is about the nature of love — the use of the word, the conventional place of so-called love in marriage and courtship, its fickleness and its perpetuity.

'Love-birds, a pair of love-birds', says Ellen the maid, speaking of the Grimes parents.

'Does that mean we are love-children?' asks nine-year-old Alice. Ellen laughs at this, with its implications of illegitimacy. She explains, 'Love is the same as anything else in the world, it's all right in its own place — *and* in moderation'.

The narrator then takes up the tale and adds: 'It was a great town for love — in its way. And the Grimes' parlour was what you might call the Temple of Love'. In the first page three points of view, those of Ellen, the child Alice and the narrator, have been put forward. We are then shown conventional courtship in the days of Matthias' youth. The word 'love' has only to be mentioned and it sends innuendoes echoing round the room. Couples are linked together 'till a fine mesh of compromise was woven around them'. Is this mesh love?

When Matthias and Alicia marry the narrator inserts another caustic comment purporting to reproduce prosaic town opinion: 'Starting straight into marriage without a honeymoon was like starting Lent without Shrove Tuesday'. Alicia and Matthias, however, remain, unusually attached. Alicia has the same bird-like fragility as Flora in 'The Becker Wives', the same ethereality. 'Poor bird', says the narrator, 'she never made a nest in the heart of her children', none of whom inherit her qualities, and soon Alicia dies.

The remaining third of the story tells of Matthias' reactions to her death. Matthias is sustained by one idea, to erect a suitable memorial to his dead wife and perpetuate the spirit of their attachment. The family discussion on the relative merits of granite, marble or limestone forms an extended reflection on the impossibility of incorporating love into any physical shape, least of all in a cemetery. Alice is by now old enough to tell her father sharply as he stands beside the grave: 'You can't make her live for ever, no matter what you do. And after all, she was only an ordinary woman. She wasn't an Egyptian queen!'

Cleopatra is the echo of another great love which has become an embodiment of erroneous belief in those who, like Alice, are unaware of the circumstances behind the original comparison. Alice stands then 'irresolute' in the moonlight and hears the woman's voice in a high, timeless note, calling her children home. She returns in memory to her own childhood in which Ellen, not her mother, has warned her about Mad Mary, the same embodiment of erroneous belief used to perpetuate a past situation, so that the unseen woman's transference of Mad Mary to 'Alicia Grimes will get you', is the final ironic thrust.[5] Will her mother's character be falsified in the same way? And if her parents' love were exclusive, so that it now remains only as a memory inside her father's head, can it have been true love at all? For in the family love 'was all kept in their mother's room, and only their father had the key'.

Though these Grimes stories are not supposed to represent a consecutive series of events there is a certain cyclic unity to the group. Birth and death of feeling in the relationships of these closely associated human beings, the flecting appearance of that radiance which is called love, also finds its parallel in the birth and death of the body. In the first story of the group, 'The Visit to the Cemetery', Liddy and Alice visit their mother's grave, situated in the old friary cemetery which figures so frequently in Mary Lavin's work and in *The House in Clewe Street*. It must surely have been an impressive place for the author in her childhood.

Liddy and Alice are there from a sense of duty. They get through 'what might almost at some previous date have been decided upon as their mother's ration' of prayers, and they ascribe human feelings to the remains. 'Poor mother', cried Liddy, 'I can't help thinking how much nicer and cleaner it would have been for her in the new cemetery!', for there human bones are never found accidentally disinterred by a badger. The love for their mother has been replaced by a vague pity and they are much more concerned with living and the 'intoxicating' thought of their future husbands. The group of Grimes stories starts and ends with the death of Alicia Grimes and her death is a part of her life, but after it she will be remembered only by the feelings she has aroused in life which remain in the memories of her family. The most enduring of these memories is the intensity of love, never yet experienced in its fullness by these two young girls. They think the intoxication of love may be found in marriage, for love to them is still almost entirely a physical state.

Has love a place? Can it be moderated, doled out, as it were, by the spoonful? Is love, like the body, inevitably subject to disintegration and decay, or does it endure beyond the grave? The author implies that most people misinterpret love, by using the term too lightly or by restricting its meaning to physical attraction. Mary Lavin was searching for the full meaning of love in this Grimes group of stories.

The mature and interestingly diverse novella 'One Summer' carries the contradictory aspects of love, and the difficulty of defining its exact nature, a little further. This story continues the tale of Vera who in 'What's wrong with Aubretia?' had given up marrying Alan in order to stay with her ageing father. When the story opens she has just seen Alan off at the pier en route to Australia; that same night her father is taken ill. Throughout the story Vera is torn between her love for her difficult father — with his 'black looks, and his fits of black, black silence', who also doses himself with cascara and treacle which he calls black-jack, and retches up black bile — and her love for Alan, receding from her life on the ship. She reminds herself of the 'miracles of love' her father performed in her mother-less childhood. As in all Lavin stories Vera reverts in memory to past events in order to underline the emotional feelings she is presently experiencing. The story also fills in some of the background not mentioned in 'What's Wrong with Aubretia?'. Significantly in this later story there is no mention of social difference between the couple and the emotional complications in this second longer story have far wider implications, for there are multiple themes woven round the father's attitudes and Vera and Alan are much more deeply revealed.

Vera's letter to Alan on board ship, telling him of her

father's illness, also illustrates her difficult role as a woman. All the ties of duty and affection bind her to her father. He had selfishly clung to her and disparaged her relationship with Alan so that her love straddles the two of them.

Rita, the flippant young nurse, provides an amusing foil to Vera's character. Rita brings warmth and liveliness into the dreary house and uses her charm to create mutual attraction but when she goes on holiday the old nurse who replaces her is quite different. Vera enters the sick room. 'The old nurse and her patient were both awake, but although they were not speaking Vera felt as if she were intruding. It was as if they were communicating in some way beyond her understanding. These unspoken messages were deep and meaningful. How could she ever have been so mistaken as to think that life had ebbed from this room? Dying too was a part of life.'

This intuitive realisation of Vera's is carried further when she notices that her father's sense of reality has altered until, 'it was the old life of health and normality in which he could not believe', so that when she tells him Alan has found another girl he replies: 'What matter'. One day, he says, her memory of Alan will be similar to his memory of her mother. They each ponder on the meaning of love, on whether or not it extends into any state of being beyond the grave. Otherwise, cries Vera, what would be the meaning of love?

The father will enter the black hole of the grave, even as Bedelia re-entered the interior of the smelly cab, both looking for a radiance they had once known, and recognise as superior in feeling to anything they have subsequently experienced, though they may not have realised this at the time. A fleeting knowledge of the existence of such a feeling elevates the human being to a plane above the physical when he is alive, so may not such a feeling be transcendent of the body? But should this feeling be called love, or can love only exist mutually between two persons on the same plane? Has Vera's love for Alan ceased to exist directly he loves another in the same way as her father's love for her mother ceased to exist when he dies? These are the questions behind the story.

The dominance of the father over his motherless daughter is repeated in another recent story, 'Asigh', in which the father dies and the story consists of the daughter's retrospective revision 'of the long imprisonment of her life with him'. The father crippled his daughter in a moment of rage and spoilt her chance of marriage. This is symbolic of the fact that for the female love may only come if she is physically attractive. The father still thinks of women primarily as breeders of the next generation. He is largely in control of his daughter's destiny and she accepts this.

For all these women characters love is very important, if often misinterpreted. It may be based on a romantic dream, a faded memory, or be expressed in action. That mention of love occurs most frequently in relation to marriage is in contradiction to the author's often cynical treatment of marriage as an escape, a convention or a convenience, looked at from the point of view of the past, present and future. Memories of love may take on as romantic a tinge as projections of a future romance, whereas married love being lived in the present tends to be prosaically hedged by drying nappies or smelly feet. In 'The Mouse', another story which reverts to the days of Nora Lavin's youth, the girl narrator's mother says: 'Oh, the past is a queer place surely! I think, sometimes, it's like what we're told to believe Heaven is like, with no marriage, and no giving in marriage only love. I mean the bodily memories die away and all you remember is the love. If it weren't for that, the pain of love would be unbearable'.

After Mary Lavin was widowed her treatment of these themes takes on a greater maturity. Emotionally she has now moved out of the world of her own youth and that in which the emotional reactions of older persons were based on her mother's rather than her own memories and experiences. In 'Heart of Gold', first published in 1964 but written in the earlier manner, there is an ironic treatment of love and marriage in which past and present are brought face to face. Middle-aged Lucy's eventual marriage to her early sweetheart, the widower Sam, is shown as a flat, quiet affair of which the bunch of snowdrops pinned to Lucy's lapel is a suitable symbol. The self-centred Sam hopes God will spare Mona, his first wife, from looking down from heaven until she can see Lucy giving him appetising meals. The most amusing passage is the account of their honeymoon train journey at which Mona is present in spirit, and Lucy thinks: 'Was this the constancy to which she had clung? Like the moon, it had two faces; on one side hers, and on the other Mona's!' Hand-cuffed by the marriage ring to Sam she must leave her romantic dreams behind. She is committed to being real at last. Lucy, like many other women in these stories, marries for the wrong reasons.

In 1960 with 'In a Café' Mary Lavin produced her first autobiographical story about the experience of widowhood. This was followed a few years later by 'In the Middle of the Fields' and 'The Cuckoo-Spit', both about the widow Vera Traske living on a farm in Meath, whose dead husband is Richard. Mary Lavin is the Mary of 'In a Cafe' and the Vera Traske in these and other stories is a projection of herself.

'In a Café' is an example of a delicately elusive and intricate story built round three characters meeting in a simple situation. Mary comes from Meath to Dublin for the day to meet Maudie, younger and also widowed. The second and third paragraphs set the scene:

It was a place she had only recently found, and she dropped in often, whenever she came up to Dublin. She hated to go anywhere else now. For one thing, she knew that she would be unlikely ever to have set foot in it if Richard were still alive. And this knowledge helped to give her back a semblance of the identity she lost willingly in marriage, but lost doubly, and unwillingly, in widowhood.

Not that Richard would have disliked the café. It was the kind of place they went to when they were students. Too much water had gone under the bridge since those days, though. Say what you liked, there was something faintly snobby about a farm in Meath, and together she and Richard would have been out of place here. But it was a different matter to come here alone. There could be nothing — oh, nothing — snobby about a widow. Just by being one, she fitted into this kind of café. It was an unusual little place. She looked around.

When Mary Lavin says she identifies with this character it should not be assumed that their attitudes are identical, because often a writer will project herself reacting in an imaginary fashion. This widow Mary implicitly criticises all those women who allow marriage to detract from their individuality and who mould their opinions and their social dignity round those or that expressed, or acquired, by their husbands. It is, nevertheless, a situation that might well not have occurred to the author before she had herself experienced widowhood, even though she had often criticised the dependent spinster in earlier stories such as 'Miss Holland'. It is also a complex sociological point, as sharing one's life with another necessarily entails some degree of adaptation, if not complete reciprocal identification. The story again shows the social status of marriage as superior to that of the single woman.

The woman's social and economic status both having been enhanced by marriage she suffers both loss of status and self-confidence when widowed. Mary is here less confident than Maudie, the young and beautiful widow, married only a year, whose baby is being raised by her parents and who already looks upon re-marriage as inevitable. Maudie 'knew a thing or two about men' and her sex appeal makes Mary envious. The instinctive reactions of the two females are played out in the presence of the male artist in the background, whom they both ignore but of whom they are both, as females, conscious.

Alongside these instinctive reactions and Mary's later behaviour in the story when she runs away from the artist's door, is her serious question. She is still an unwilling widow, insecure physically, emotionally and socially. She asks herself: '. . . if she could not remember him, at will, what meaning had time at all? What use was it to have lived in the past, if behind us it fell away so sheer? In the hours of his death, for her it was part of the pain that she knew this would happen'. So she is filled by a nameless panic. She had to construct a new identity as a single person. Looking at the picture of roses she stops herself wondering what Richard would have said: 'So what would *she* say about them? She would say — she would'. She cannot yet formulate her own opinion.

At a rational level this widow wants to be independent but at emotional and instinctive levels she still hankers after the approval, admiration and support of the male. Social convention and all the clichés of widowhood conflict with instinct. Maudie's pressing her hand to her breasts expresses physical anguish, sexual and emotional repression. Maudie's manner to the artist shows this even more clearly. When they leave the café Mary goes off with the artist's address. Running through her mind is an undercurrent of thought about him. How should she interpret his invitation? Was there an emotional reason for his interest in them? Was it artistic vanity, or commercial optimism? His evident loneliness and shabbiness had appealed to the maternal instincts of both women but men rarely regard women of a similar age group paternally. This women learn very early on.

Mary's mind flits constantly from tangibles to intangibles. At one moment she sees herself reflected in the mirror, and tells herself that her 'dowdy, lumpish, and unromantic figure vouched for her spiritual integrity'. But her outward appearance is quite at variance with her instinctive urges and these again conflict with her socially conditioned responses. Her approach to the artist's house is an escapade in which heart takes precedence over head and results in more internal confusion. Her feelings of guilt and shame are logically untenable. With whom can she speak the language of the heart save with Richard whom she has lost? Richard was the only one who assuaged her instinctive feelings. The fact that in the end she recalls Richard's face at will for the first time in two years is a symbol of her own separate, reborn identity, and with this she has 'no more than got back her rights'.

'In the Middle of the Fields' shows the widowed Vera Traske living with her children on her Meath farm. This story is less complex but the significance of widowhood is again explored at logical, emotional and instinctive levels.

And yet she was less lonely for him here in Meath than elsewhere. Anxieties by day, and cares, and at night vague, nameless fears — these were the stones across the mouth of the tomb. But who understood that? They thought she hugged tight every memory she had of him. What did they know about memory? What was it but another name for dry love and barren longing?

Her conversation with Bartley Crossen, who comes to arrange about topping the grass, and returns late at night to discuss changing the arrangement, well conveys the slightly patronising, or protective attitude of the male towards a helpless woman. But when Crossen's primitive male urge is aroused in the dark, to his subsequent embarrassment, she is not afraid of him in the least. This woman has achieved an independent identity but she is still insecure. A woman on her own can be more emotionally self-contained than a man, at the cost of a certain personal softness, but remains physically and socially dependent on the strength and assertiveness associated with the masculine image.

The volume *In the Middle of the Fields* is dedicated to Michael Scott, S.J., and published two years before Mary Lavin remarried. All the stories in the volume deal with male/female relationships from different points of view. Can human love be based on a romantic memory of what once was, or might have been, or is this just 'barren longing'? Mary Lavin shows time passing but her characters remain obstinately conscious of their past. Everything is not forgotten. Memory can, as for Vera in 'One Summer' or Miss Lomas in 'The Mock Auction', hold an illusionary sway over the present, creating a fantastic actuality which is pitiful or ridiculous according to circumstances. We are all conditioned by the past and must make choices how we shape the future. To what extent should the past dominate or colour our lives, loves and feelings? In 'Heart of Gold' Sam asks Lucy, 'Guilt for what, Lucy? Is it for the past?'

In 'The Cuckoo-Spit', another story in this volume, the widow Vera Traske is sociologically a world away from the dependent women shown in Mary Lavin's early work, and there are further insights into the difficult role of the widow.

The Vera in this story is nervous after dark. Her children are not mentioned but after four years of widowhood she is still emotionally insecure. The young Fergus gives her both reassurance and affection. His coming causes her to question the meaning of love and happiness, both of which in her moments of defeat she thinks have left her life for ever. She is also concerned about the falsification of her husband's memory. She blames him 'for leaving a void that no one less than him could fill'. The love in their marriage had been rooted in full companionship as well as sex.

Only a very lonely middle-aged woman would reveal herself as fully as Vera does to a much younger man whose persistent attention is flattering but clumsy, and the character of Fergus never really comes to life. His youth conveys, nevertheless, the impossibility of putting the clock back. He provides a foil to her musings about the dead Richard, and a focus for her thoughts.

Instinct in this story is again used to orchestrate: Vera enjoys the physical presence and confidences of a male; what she calls the trivia of their conversation creates the dialogue but the real purpose of the story is contained in the slight shifts of thought and feeling shown in the narrative passages. Can there be friendship without sex between man and woman? Vera is not sure; perhaps there are only two valid relationships — blood and passion; but Fergus helps Vera in the quest of trying to find herself, differently repeated from 'In a Café':

When he died, I knew I had to get back to being that other person again, just as he, when he was dying, had to get back to being the kind of person he was before he met me. Standing beside him in those last few minutes, I felt he was trying to drag himself free of me. Can you understand that? Does it make any sense to you?

In fact she is a different person because of her married experience. Her 'pallid belief in a life beyond the grave' has been quenched but she cannot commit herself to love another, let alone a much younger man with an emotional maturity so unformed compared to her own. Vera illustrates this by her analogy about the lights viewed from Howth Head. The eventual social effect of marrying a young man impedes her instinctive physical response, and in addition she is not sure that sex can overcome their differences.

In the end it is Vera who takes the initiative and breaks off the relationship before it has, as Fergus wishes, been given any physical expression. She sees that a couple cannot be self-sufficient. What others think is bound to affect them. The inner and outer aspects of reality must, for true happiness, always be held in balance. It would always be Vera who took the lead, and as a woman she does not feel prepared to do that.

The highly aware Vera Traske of this story can no longer view love romantically. She longs for male companionship but to a young man sex is the necessary preliminary doorway, and there is an ironic note contained in the contradictory remark at the end of the story. Vera says: ' "I sometimes think love has nothing to do with people at all", her voice was tired. "It's like the weather!" Suddenly she turned to face him, "But isn't it strange that a love that was unrealised should have . . ." ', and she leaves the sentence unfinished.

If love between man and woman can only be 'realised' by sexual contact and yet exists in some way before this has taken place, what is this unrealised love? Is it merely a feeling that deepens self-awareness, giving both joy and pain? These tantalising questions hang in the air at the end of the story. It is also evident that the middle-aged but still attractive widow has an uneasy social role to fill. In the small town life depicted in the

Athenry stories the widow fitted into a much surer place, if she could live by acceptable social norms, with intimate male companionship confined to members of her own family. But if the widow wishes to become an independent personality she has to forge herself a new identity, a role which fits uneasily into accepted social patterns.

In 'Trastevere' Mrs Traske the novelist, 'widowed young herself, but having enough good sense not to make public by marriage a second, late but deeply satisfying relationship', has her own concept of love and this does not include a woman dominating men. Her description of the curious *ménage à trois* in this story has a strong air of distaste about it. Della's husband Simon, and the young poet Paul are both financially dependent on Della who first appears to Mrs Traske in the phallic image of a maypole, festooned with ribbons, which, as they gyrate, bind the young men closer and closer to her. This is Mary Lavin's only story about a 'liberated' woman upon whom the men are emotionally and financially dependent; but there are signs in the story that Simon is starting to rebel against her brittle control, so that by the end the usurper of the maypole shrinks: ' . . . was it possible that Della wasn't strong at all — that she had all the time been taking strength, not giving it as the young men thought?' Does she commit suicide to escape from the dominating role she has forced upon herself? This leads Mrs Traske to re-examine her own concept of love at the end of the story where, in what must be largely personal musing from the author, she thinks about her male friend:

> She did not see much point in getting married at their age, when they had not much left to give each other, and he had shaken his head in disagreement.
>
> "At least we do not diminish each other", he

said.

Were they making a mistake, she wondered, she and Mack? In spite of how often they thrashed things out and discarded the idea of marrying — laughed at the mere notion — perhaps after all . . .

For the mature couple companionship and love are in-extricably interwoven and their dependency must be mutual. The sexual side gives external expression to the quality of love which pre-exists and surpasses it. This is again a question of holding in balance the inner reality of love and its outward manifestation.

In real life her motherhood is very important to Mary Lavin but woman's role as wife or partner takes precedence over motherhood in her stories, though she treated motherhood at length in her novel *Mary O'Grady,* written when the raising of her children took up the principal part of her day.

The worried widow/mother, Vera Traske, reappears with her brood in another partially autobiographical story, 'Villa Violetta', and there is one other story about motherhood, 'Happiness', the title story of the volume dedicated to her daughters Elizabeth and Caroline.

The mother, also named Vera, in this story seems to be a mixture of Mary Lavin herself and her own mother, and the grandmother's character is borrowed from mother figures of the author's youth. The narrator is an ironic mingling of her own, and her daughter's points of view.

The mother image is here one of persistently un-selfish service and sacrifice, unlike that of the grand-mother who prides herself on being imperious and whose image in the young narrators' minds 'was a complicated mixture of valiance and defeat'. The mother's perpetual search for happiness means making others happy. This is 'the mystery of the light that still radiated from her', a light that was evidently dimmed for a while after her husband's death. The detail here included is once more a personal writing-out of some harrowing memories on the author's part.

Happiness in this story is struggled for by a positive refusal to accept either defeat or the conventional attitudes of society when these involve a negative approach. The batlike mourners in black are 'not living in a real world at all; they belong to a ghostly world where life was easy; all one had to do was sit and weep. It takes effort to push back the stone from the mouth of the tomb and walk out'. The treatise on the nature of happiness is wound in and out of the plot. The girls try to define this happiness of their mother's. Is it, they ask, health, strength or high spirits? But happiness is never defined. It is the delicate balance, different to each person, achieved by giving and receiving in equal proportion.

The widowed mother tries to defeat loneliness within by perpetual activity, and for her children the happiness she clings to and by which she sets such store is only evident when she is combining love and activity by working in her garden. It is here that she is finally found unconscious.

The story expresses a possible extension of one of Mary Lavin's selves — if she had allowed herself to become obsessed by material anxieties of family and farm; if she had not had her writing as an outlet; if she had remained 'only a mother'. The lack of happiness shown by so many of her women characters is because they become entangled in a web of social convention and material detail which love's radiance cannot penetrate.

Mary Lavin's female characters and narrators show men from many different points of view, the clumsy young lover, the romantic beau, the domineering or weak husband or father, the self-centred career man, the vacillator. Men make demands. It is important for women to please them. Many of her women are social appendages who live half lives; others, particularly in her later stories, start emerging as fully fledged individuals and widowhood is shown as painfully forcing a woman to do this. Marriage, an enduring relationship, may be a hell or a haven. Its religious significance is rarely mentioned. It is viewed as a social institution and as such open to abuse. Marriage is the most intimate human relationship but not always based on love. Love is, in any case, like the birds which figure so often in the stories, ever on the wing and once caged may not sing. Its appearance endows the possessor with a fleeting radiance which is comparatively rare. More often love remains as a memory in the mind, an ideal to be blindly and mistakenly striven for.

An interwoven series of dichotomies form the background to her stories, the practical and the ideal; the external and the internal; head versus heart; logic versus instinct and emotion; social conditioning confronted by primal desire, and of all these male and female are part. Mary Lavin's women are most often subservient to, or at least heavily dependent on, their male partner. When they dominate, as does conniving Bodelia, or Della in 'Trastevere', unhappiness results. Yet when we look at stories told from the male point of view it is surprising how often the male narrator is either hen-pecked, or a celibate. The only story with a male narrator showing a happy husband is 'My Molly', an ironic treatment by the simple first person narrator of his wife's reactions which ends: 'What I sometimes wonder is, will I ever understand her: My Molly?'

Mary Lavin's first story about a celibate male was 'Love is for Lovers' (1942), in which Mathew Simmins, who began to think about marriage 'at the non-committal age of forty-four', is a cold, meticulously obsessive but straightforward person. He is contrasted with Mrs Cooligan the 'sonsy', warm, careless subtle widow. The story centres round the conflict between heat and passion, coldness, detachment and death, and it has the allegorical undertone of a morality tale based on the medieval humours. Mathew ponders on the differences between men and women but, 'he assumed that, great and small, they were differences he would never really fully explore'. In spite of all Mrs Cooligan's attempts to entice him by the route to a man's heart through his stomach, Mathew refuses to be trapped. His virginal fastidiousness makes him shrink from even contemplating the physical intimacies involved in marriage, a foretaste of which he sees in the way Mrs Cooligan treats her dog. He wants everything 'to be cool and clear'. He feels the simmering warmth of the widow as a smothering, stifling condition. In his icy self-sufficiency he is already half dead.

Mary Lavin's first henpecked husband character appears in 'At Sallygap', a richly nuanced story which a contemporary reviewer likened to Sean O'Casey's work,[6] but the tone of which seems more reminiscent of Joyce's 'A Little Cloud'.[7]

As the narrator of the story Manny does not at first appear in his henpecked role but exudes self-confidence as he recounts the story of why he has never left Ireland to the young man on the bus. The smashed fiddle, like the burnt poetry in 'A Happy Death', symbolises the end of Manny's dreams. His original ambitions have been quashed in a poky backstreet Dublin shop.

The second Manny appears in the middle section of the story where he is walking along alone, incongruously bowler-hatted in the country. Away from his normal environment he is possessed by a feeling of recklessness and a desire to escape even as far as Liverpool. With a bit of luck he might make his expenses at a race meeting and 'that would shut Annie's mouth'. He is able to view his life with a certain detachment. In his mind's eye he sees his slatternly wife, 'giving off old shaffoge with any shawley who came the way and had an hour, or maybe two hours, to spare'.

One might doubt that Manny has quite the perceptivity he is credited with in the fine description of seedy Dublin which follows. And as so often in Mary Lavin's early work the author spoils it by intervening at the end of this middle section to make her point:

> At last he had found his real escape from the sordidness of the life he led, and perhaps in time the seed of sensitiveness that had lain sterile in his heart through his bleak and unnatural spring and summer might have had a rare and wonderful autumn flowering. There are gentle souls who take nothing from their coarse rearing, and less from their chance schooling, but who yet retain a natural sensitivity, and sometimes it flowers, as Manny's did, in the hills.

In the final section of the story the third Manny is shown back home with his wife:

> Marriage had been an act of unselfishness on Manny's part. He married Annie because he thought that was what would make her happy, and he was content to give up his own freedom for that object. She, however, had not thought of marriage as anything but a means of breaking the monotony. And she had soon found it a greater monotony than the one she had fled from, and, unlike the other, it was no anteroom of hope leading to something better.

Having been shown Manny as he once was, and Manny as he might have been, we now see Manny as he is, married to a frustrated virago whose bottled-up abilities have turned to fantasy and sloth, and whose energy can only find expression in hatred.

In this, one of Mary Lavin's seminal stories, there are many layers of implication which will strike a reader according to his personal perceptions and experiences.[8] One critic sees a female character such as Annie as a devourer of male frailty.[9] Another critic of this story points out that Manny's only salvation is to re-discover nature.[10] Both interpretations are justified. The atmosphere of place in 'At Sallygap' is particularly vivid. Its over-riding theme is the hell created by a close relationship between individuals who, from a mixture of temperamental and sociological causes, are mutually incompatible.[11]

There are dominant 'masculine' women as there are retiring 'feminine' men like Danny, Manny and Mathew Simmins. Though western society, in general, now takes a limited cognisance of this fact, inherited social patterns of reactions remain and are reflected here. Annie finds Manny lacks 'manliness'. Manny only 'disgusts to himself' because he does not project the masculine image she would like him to have, and, with Mary Lavin's usual ironic twist, the joke is on Annie. It is she who is the more disgusting of the two.

Frank O'Connor said:

A woman cannot afford to caricature herself as a man may do, and if she does, she is made to pay for it. It is a drawback to the Irish woman writer. But, on the other hand, a woman's ideas of success and failure need not necessarily be the same as a man's. No man need regard himself as a failure if he has failed with women, but a woman does so almost invariably if she has failed with men. All through Mary Lavin's stories one is aware of a certain difference in values which finally resolves itself into an almost Victorian attitude to love and marriage, an attitude one would be tempted to call old-fashioned if it did not make the attitude of so many famous modern women writers seem dated.[12]

When O'Connor wrote those lines Edna O'Brien's *A Pagan Place* (London 1970) and *Mother Ireland* (London 1976) had not been written. Such self-revelation is no longer a drawback to the courageous Irish woman writer who has, like the women in Mary Lavin's later stories, increasingly become a person in her own right, rather than merely a woman who is supposed to play second fiddle.

It is true that a woman's ideas of success and failure need not be the same as a man's, though there are now many women whose idea of success is not tied exclusively to success with men. Most of the earlier Lavin stories are based on the old feminine route to social success, through status acquired by marriage, and only a few of her female characters show that love and mutual compatibility can sublimate difficult social circumstances and create success of the heart, more valuable and enduring than that based on society's norms. Her marriages are lifelong commitments for better or worse, and therefore have an element of fatality about them. The conventional male idea of success, through doing rather than being, is less explored in her work, for as in the novels of Jane Austen, most of her male characters are approached along the lines of their private lives, rather than through their professional relationships. Occasionally a character such as Christopher in 'The Haymaking', Alan in 'What's Wrong with Aubretia?', Tod Mallon in 'Asigh', will show that his centre of interest lies elsewhere, the only other exceptions being priest characters such as the canon in 'A Pure Accident' and 'The Shrine', and the male narrators of 'A Woman Friend' and 'A Memory'.

This stress on the personal rather than the professional, and the preponderantly domestic themes

among groups of people all adhering to a stable moral
ethos, in which marriage or talk of it plays such a large
part, does indeed give the impression of an attitude
similar to that associated with Victorian writers.

With the recent wider understanding of sex roles, the
dichotomy based on sex shown in early Lavin work has
evolved to become rather a dichotomy based on perception of different types of sensibility. These types
may coincide with or overlap sex differences, and her
characters have become increasingly less stereotyped in
the male or female image.

Though no man need regard himself as a failure if
he has failed with women, men who do fail with women
are not shown by Mary Lavin in a favourable light.
The difference between a man's own image of success
and how differently he may be regarded by a woman are
treated in two stories about platonic relationships 'A
Woman Friend' and 'A Memory', written twenty years
apart, from which it is also interesting to see how the
social evolution of the female state has affected the
author's treatment of this theme.

'A Woman Friend' was extensively revised from its
original 1951 version for Volume II of the collected
stories published in London in 1974. In the later version
the complicated unfolding of the train of events has
been given greater clarity and Dr Lew Anderson's pride
in his professional abilities is more heavily stressed by
the addition of a new passage about his operating
brilliance.

The overt turning point of this story, the death of the
patient, is a device used to bring out the reactions of the
doctor to an emotional situation which shakes him out
of his normal professional complacency and causes him
to take stock of himself and his life; thus revealing a
singularly unaware, egotistical person. Because
Anderson's picture of himself, gradually built up as the
story unfolds, shows such a different private person

from his public image there is an ironic incongruity between the man as he hopes to appear and the man as he really is. The author thereby invites the reader to judge this man's actions. The principal inference is that self-sufficiency leads to frigidity and stunted emotional development, however successful a person may be in professional terms.

Anderson puts his medical career first with scalpel-like scrupulosity. He has put up his plate in the best part of Dublin. He is professionally impeccable, hard-working and conscientious. In his work he goes far beyond the call of duty but more from the desire to impress than from altruism. 'It wasn't enough to get to the top; you had to stay there; and as far as he could make out, to stay there meant ruling out a lot of things that other men took to be theirs by right. So many of his contemporaries had fallen back into mediocrity for the sake of bodily comfort. It was usually marriage, of course'.

Anderson's only intimate friend is Bina who runs the boarding house where he once lived back in his student days. He uses Bina's basement sitting room as a refuge when tired after work. He relaxes there in womblike warmth. 'She never made any demands on him at any time, not even the smallest'.

Marriage with Bina would not be good for his professional advancement, so he takes all he can from her giving nothing in return. Anderson believes his only weakness is a tendency to fall asleep suddenly; a weakness which nearly brings his reputation into doubt when he sleeps in his car outside his rooms and fails to answer the telephone calling him urgently back to the hospital. Upset by this possible slur on his character, Anderson seeks comfort from Bina. He feels a childlike desire to lay his head on the bosom of her flannel nightgown when he sees her thus dressed, and without spectacles for the first time. He mentally associates her naked face with the 'indignity' of marriage and the 'pitiful exposure of sex'. His final offer of marriage to Bina, which he later regrets, is made for reasons of expediency. As a doctor he is successful, as a human being he is a failure. It is not his physical coldness which shocks but his warped emotional response and self-centredness. We are not told whether or not Bina accepts his offer, though Anderson takes it for granted that she will. If she refused he would blame her for lack of ambition, not for loving him too much.

This man does not regard himself as a failure, because he has failed with women, neither does Bina appear to regard him as such. She plays the traditional female wet nurse role, a combination mother/sister kept firmly in her place. This man has failed to mature as a fully developed person. His heart is permanently asleep for he is obsessed by professional success. He is not afraid of love as Mathew is in 'Love is for Lovers', he simply has no time to love anyone but himself.

In 'A Memory' Mary Lavin attempted a longer and much more intricate story on a similar theme. The male narrator is an elderly academic, James, a research professor who lives a secluded life writing in his Meath cottage. 'His work filled his life as it filled his day. He seldom had ocasion to go up to the University. When he went up it was to see Myra, and then only on impulse if for some reason work went against him'.

Myra is a professional translator who lives in a Dublin mews flat, intellectual and warmhearted but not domesticated. Emmy, the third character in the story, never appears. James once loved her in his youth — the only time he ever loved — and this love, remaining in his memory, gives the story its title. In the same way as the old father in 'One Summer', and Matthias in 'Loving Memory' allow a past love or happiness to monopolise feelings, or serve as an emotional retreat, this memory is once again given a pejorative inference. It must be

supposed that Mary Lavin treats this theme so often
because an awareness of its danger occurred in her own
life, and Mrs Traske, the widow, is shown making
strenuous efforts to escape from the imprisonment of
memory. For though memories can enrich one's life
they should not dominate subsequent behaviour.

At least James, unlike Anderson, has once loved, but
both men suffer from what T. P. Coogan has called 'a
kind of Sean O'Oedipus complex — a shrinking from sex
as something shameful and a treachery to the maternal
and sisterly love which is so strong a force in Irish
family life . . . .' In these stories, as in others in which
the female single state or the effects of celibacy in the
priesthood are the subject, Mary Lavin shows that
'astringency in her treatment of celibacy' remarked
upon by Frank O'Connor.

Mary Lavin here explores whether there can be real
intimacy between the sexes without full physical
commitment, but she does so through two male
characters each of whom develops a selfish platonic
relationship with a woman entirely on his own terms. In
neither story does the woman visit the man's house. In
both stories the woman waits on the man and is used by
him as a maternal or sisterly pillow.

The first and last parts of 'A Memory' are narrated
by James and the short central section by Myra. There
is ironic contrast between their two points of view.
Looking back to his meeting with Emmy he thinks:

> . . . it was as if a fiery circle had been blazed around
> them, allowing no way out for either until he, James,
> in the end had to close his eyes and break through,
> not caring about the pain as long as he got outside
> again. Because Myra was right. Marriage would have
> put an end to his academic career. For a man like
> him it would have been suffocating.

James likes Myra because of the 'uniquely undemanding quality of her feeling for him'. He likes the masculine air of her flat but also her femininity, the scent from her clothes, and the fact that she is always available when he arrives without warning. He admires her intellect and her economic independence which present no threat to him. For James the 'wifey' things of life are distasteful. The thought of dribbling children and smelly nappies is abhorrent and nauseating. He likes the household routine to be done by another without fuss. Myra therefore orders food from a café. After eating he likes to sit and stroke her hand. Myra treats him with a mixture of cajolery and protectiveness, and he has come to believe that 'a man and woman could enter into a marriage of minds'. Their relationship seems to him to be one of equality not dependence.

When Myra takes over the narrative, however, we see James' impression of her is erroneous. After ten years of friendship Myra is disappointed in him, and a recent hysterectomy operation has affected her emotional susceptibility. James is inconsiderate but she is partly to blame for 'when they'd first met she had sensed deep down in him a capacity for the normal feelings of friendship and love. Yet throughout the years she had consistently deflected his feelings away from herself and consistently encouraged him to seal them off. Tonight it seemed that his emotional capacity was completely dried up. Despair overcame her. She'd never change him now. He was fixed in his faults, cemented into his barren way of life'. When she gives way to an hysterical outburst James is scandalised and leaves at once. Myra has revealed her true self at last but he cannot accept her on her terms, only on his.

Their marriage of minds is not enough. True friendship, let alone marriage, must be based on mutual feeling and concern. In spite of James's intelligence and rational argument he shows no feeling for Myra. His 'ideals' are ironically revealed to be seeing only 'what was best, and best preserved, in the other'. Reality, such as the unattractive process of ageing, is sordid. A lie makes James feel sick but he lives in a perpetual grey world of reticent half-truth. In the end he dies in the dark woods, looking for a gleam of light in the sky to direct him, stumbling round the home of the woman he had once loved, and falling, his mouth full of rotted leaves — dead. James, though professionally eminent, has failed with women because, like Anderson, he lacks heart. He is a success in his own eyes but not in Myra's. The social evolution of the female has granted Myra independence and professional status yet without a man's love she feels 'denatured' and 'deprived'. Woman's truth of the heart is just as important as man's truth of the head, but does not modern society set too much store by the latter?

Myra, by conforming to the cerebral marriage imposed by James, has perpetuated an emotional and physical celibacy destructive to both of them because it forbids a full expansion of feeling and stunts a part of the personality.

In the lives portrayed in the earlier stories platonic relationships between the sexes would have been unthinkable, but Mary Lavin shows that neither friendship nor marriage work if they are based merely on social convenience. Marriage can cause a woman to submerge her personality completely, as celibacy can encourage a self-sufficient egoism. Too much self-sacrifice from Myra is as destructive as too little from James. It is again a question of balance. The rough and the smooth, the sordid and the enthralling must form part of any full relationship.

Anderson and James both use a woman for their own needs but ignore the needs of the woman. Bina and Myra are partly to blame for they indulge the men. The women in both stories are shown as more intuitively and emotionally developed than the men. It would seem from the second story that with the increase of feminine independence women have a greater responsibility to remain true to their feminine state and should not try to ape the attitudes and ways of life of men. Myra reflects an aspect of the modern woman's uncertainty about the female role in society.[15]

Mary Lavin's treatment of these themes implies criticism of those whose priorities do not include love, because they misunderstand its nature. She reveals her concern by setting so many stories in the heart of an intimate human relationship, the frail and erroneously motivated structure of which is ironically revealed. Love and marriage have inner and outer aspects and the institution which formalises and is a symbol of the love bond does not necessarily contribute anything to perpetuate the inner state. A marriage of minds without physical contact is just as sterile as a marriage of lust without mental affinity.

Marriage is a mockery if entered into only as an escape from monotony, a haven of security, to confer social status, to acquire possession of another, or to breed children. Love needs to share and to give, it expects sacrifice and creates both joy and pain. It lingers in the memory more strongly than any other human experience; it lends courage and dignity to the individual superior to that of any material state, and its radiance transforms its possessor.

Although Mary Lavin's later characters continue to misinterpret the nature of love, and minimise its importance in favour of social preoccupations, modern man and woman are shown having enhanced potential to experience love in its fullness, because they are no longer as strongly conditioned, nor as socially constrained as in the past. To take advantage of this potential, however, they must remain true to their instincts and be aware of their essentially complementary abilities.

3 Religious Conventions

Religion in the Irish Republic means catholicism and its influence is an integral part of the Irish social scene. Different illustrations of religious convention, often treated ironically, form an important theme in Mary Lavin's work which no dispassionate critic can afford to ignore. The treatment of such themes reflects the author's awareness that the transcendental is often given insufficient, or warped, human interpretation, embodied in formalistic ritual or denigrated to prescriptive rules. It is again a question of the external expression dominating, falsifying, or failing to express the inner spirit.

Mary Lavin has said: 'I am a catholic and it's important to me. I think the fate of the Church may well be in the hands of the laity . . .'[1] Speaking of her arrival as a child in Ireland, she said:

A young American child coming to a small town in Ireland, as I did, found eye-opening differences between American Catholicism and Irish Catholicism. I went to Sunday school in America, which to us has a very Protestant connotation, but it is a very Catholic

concept in America. I was suddenly thrown into a
small Irish community, and I would say that my
mother's family were very much at the mercy of
what we would now call superstition. They didn't
think for themselves, they accepted everything they
were told, and I'm sure they often misinterpreted it.
I came to a town in Ireland, the town of Athenry,
and was there only for eight months, but those eight
months made a tremendous mark on me. The place
where I was born in America was only a village, but
not very rural because in those days one of the main
roads from Boston to Providence ran through it. We
used to go to Mass in the local cinema, and if for any
reason we couldn't go to a Catholic Mass, we had a
dispensation to go to a Polish or Greek Orthodox
Mass instead — a situation unheard of in Ireland
because the need would never have arisen.[2]

She fictionalised her early impression of Irish catholic
attitudes in 'Limbo', an amusing story about the
Pastons, English protestant missionaries from Africa,
who settle in Castlerampart with their daughter Naida
aged thirteen. Naida is enrolled in the local school where
she is not permitted to attend prayers. There is an amusing exchange between Lottie White, the school
monitress, and Naida, revealing the former's ignorance.
Lottie has never heard of lay missionaries or non-
sectarian Christians who are prepared to attach themselves to any Christian denomination, and Naida's
explanation that 'God had no church when He was on
earth' does nothing to help.

Mamie Sully, with whom Naida makes friends, illustrates small town mentality, a cultural limbo in which
old books are kept in a loft over the stable. Naida is
treated by the other children as an oddity who does not
fit into the accepted social categories they take for
granted. Miss White's superior 'pity' for protestants is

interpreted by the children in rigid catechetical terms. They decide that Naida, as a benighted protestant, will not go to heaven but will remain in that waiting place of limbo until the prayers of the faithful enable her to reach the state of bliss.

Lottie says of the Pastons 'they have a Protestant look', but '. . . no one could have been called upon to define exactly what constituted the difference between a Protestant look and a Catholic look. It was a matter of instinct'.

In another story from the same period, 'The Convert', in which Naida Paston and Maimie (sic) Sully are now adults, Mary Lavin again investigates this delicate difference.[3]

Maimie Sully, who remains Naida's so-called best friend, has married Elgar, and he now runs the Sully family shop. When the story opens Naida has just died, and Elgar thinks back to when, as a Trinity College student four years before, he had boarded with the Pastons.

Maimie had then flirted with Elgar and played up the catholic-protestant difference. She had told Elgar of Naida: 'I always said that you couldn't expect her to have followers, like the rest of us, when there were no young men in the town. No young men of her own kind, I mean'. Yet when Elgar, a young man of Naida's 'own kind', appeared, Maimie had made a deliberate effort to prevent the formation of any deep relationship between them.

Elgar, entranced by Maimie, had given up his studies, Naida who loved him, and turned catholic. Maimie is still making a fool of him after four years of marriage. They have a daughter and Maimie is again pregnant but still carries on a mild flirtation with Owdie Hicks, one of her previous 'followers'. Because Maimie, Owdie and Miss Mongon, the shop assistant, are all cradle catholics there is something about their subconscious attitudes which Elgar, the convert, recognises but cannot share. Of Owdie and Maimie he thinks: 'The pusillanimity of their affair was contemptible. If there was some iniquity in them he thought he could have endured it better. And yet, in his heart, he knew that even by his contempt he wronged them, and that it was not pusillanimity that kept them from sin, but that for all their ogling and double meanings they were curiously innocent. Where had they come by this integrity? Was it bred in them, or was it inculcated in them by their religion?'

Because of this 'curious innocence' the innuendoes acceptable as such to the three catholics irritate Elgar with his inherited puritanical outlook, giving him a slightly different perception of reality from the rather more dualistic Irish catholic one. When Maimie and the others come to discuss Naida's wake the difference in attitude is further revealed. Naida may be waked in her house, but for catholics it is the law of the church that the coffin be left in the empty church all night. Maimie goes on to give the practical reasons why the body is better out of the house. She speaks in an explicit fashion which the reticent Elgar, accustomed to treat death in a more euphemistic manner, evidently finds distasteful, though Maimie appears unaware of this.

Elgar has missed his chance of a soulmate by leaving Naida, and he has no real rapport with Maimie, their inherited religious differences being only, of course, part of the reason. The only improbable aspect of the story is that Elgar, so aware of his wife's feelings and her power over him, is unable to analyse his own.

That the protestant look is identifiable also occurs in 'An Akoulina of the Irish Midlands' when the narrator wrongly takes it for granted that Andy Hackett must be the protestant because he has a lonely look. There is in this story an interplay of two unexpressed ideas in Andy's mind. If he seduces Lena, the protestant, it will somehow be less heinous than if she were a catholic, especially if his parish priest does not know about it; if she becomes pregnant her family is likely to agree to her becoming a catholic 'no matter what sacrifices had to be made'. Andy will never 'turn' and mixed marriages are frowned upon.

The juridical outweighs the charismatic. The authority of the catholic church is stressed in all Mary Lavin's early work, and her ironic treatment shows that she thinks the vital interpretation of the Christian message has been overlaid by prejudice, leading to ignorant fear and superstition in the simplest people and accentuating the material at the expense of the spiritual.[4]

Another comment on this theme appears in 'Sarah', the story of a woman with three illegitimate children, where in the first published version it says: 'If Sarah had been one to lie in bed on a Sunday morning, and miss Mass, the villagers would have shunned her, and crossed their breasts when they spoke of her. There was greater understanding in their hearts for sins against God than there was for sins against the Church. And Sarah found it easy to keep the commands of the servant of the Lord, even if she found it somewhat difficult to keep the commands of the Lord Himself'. Missing mass on a Sunday or holy day of obligation was a mortal sin, according to the rule of the church; committing adultery a mortal sin according to the ten commandments.

In 'Sunday brings Sunday' we are given long excerpts from the curate's sermons on the power of prayer. Prayer is efficacious; it is our duty to pray; prayer should not just consist of asking for favours in time of trouble. But prayer is also directly related to the after-life: 'I ask you to turn over in your minds whether it is better to get down on your knees for three minutes or to spend an eternity in the dark pit of damnation, lit only by the flames of hell; those flames that never quench. It is a terrible thought, but one which it is helpful to keep constantly before us'.

This is a similar theme, but less rhetorically expressed, to that of the sermon Stephen Dedalus listens to in *The Portrait of an Artist as a Young Man*, in which the 'ever' and 'nevers' describing hell sound a knell. The soul's wellbeing after death depends on the body's behaviour on earth; by prayer the living can obtain some remission of suffering to those in hell or limbo.

Mona, the young girl in this story, is as accustomed to sermons invoking fear, stressing sin, and the transitory mortal state, as she is to the annual ritual of devotions. She 'drinks in every word the priest utters'. Before the days of radio and television her imaginative nourishment comes almost entirely from this source. She and her mother are both pious and biddable but neither has learned to think for herself. Holy Mother Church wraps them in an innocence based on ignorance, and 'the long sermon with its familiar Latin words fell heavily on the air with the falling force of dead things'; but the question Mona really wants an answer to, she cannot articulate. If they belong to the confession box, questions must be whispered as a sin. But what is a sin? The priest never even mentions 'kissing' and that kind of thing. She thinks he should help her. The reality of temptation, sin, death and hell she hears in church is not on the same plane of reality as the hot tussle with Jimmy in the hay.

Edna O'Brien has described her own dreamy child-like state of mind whereby the love of Christ, seen as a dead body on the cross, and love as expressed by a kiss, left its instinctive inhibiting aftermath: 'One kissed the huge prone cross on Good Friday and one felt the gravity of it and gazed at the gloomy altar bereft of flowers. One kissed one's mother's sallow cheeks and thought of blancmange, now and then one secretly kissed a girl friend. A kiss was something dangerous that got born in the back of the throat, forming itself like a bud or a pearl, coming through the mouth and at last delivering itself on the lips which was in fact its shallow manifestation'.[5] The lover's kiss is never mentioned in Mary Lavin's stories. The lips of the dying are encouraged to formulate prayers not kisses.

Sean Ó Faoláin has recently added his impression of childhood memories of catholic upbringing:

> I was reared a pious, a very pious Irish Catholic boy and of this quaint religion I have two things to say. The first is to inform the people who sell detergents that there is one dye, one pigment, one stain, scar or mark that no soap in the world can wholly eradicate, and this is the experience of being filled from the age of four onward with — in the words of John Henry Newman — a profound distrust of the reality of material phenomena; an early fear that all life may be a dream and all this physical world a deception. The second thing is that while this mesmeric power is by no means the monopoly of any one religion, I do not think that any western church revels so perfervidly as the Irish Catholic Church does, or at any rate did when I was a boy, in the liquefaction of common life, the vaporisation of the mortal into the mystical, the veiling of the natural in the fumes of the supernatural, always at the expense of failing to develop the character of men as social animals. So, then, far from providing me with codes, values or rules for living in this pragmatical pig of a world, as Yeats called it, all that, so far as I could see, the Faith into which I was born offered me was a useful set of formalities, rather like a passport stamped with a lot of visas, guaranteed to get me as quickly as possible through this unpleasant world to my happy destina-

tion in the next.[6]

Though Mary Lavin might not agree with part of this analysis she seems to have been struck by a church obsessed with the outward, actual representation of the mystical, and if there was any contempt for life inculcated by her early training it emerges as an abiding concern with death, mentioned so frequently in her stories, and a restraint in the description of explicit physical detail; though this is less marked in her later work.

The actual representation or embodiment of the mystical is also expressed in her stories dealing with priests and nuns, who above all should be committed Christians. Here again Irish sociological conditioning plays its part.

To have a son or daughter a religious is not only a spiritual blessing but a social accolade, and it is against this latter aspect of the religious vocation Mary Lavin tilts her irony in three stories about nuns, 'The Nun's Mother', 'Chamois Gloves' and 'My Vocation', all three amusing, the first being by far the most intricate.

'The Nun's Mother',[7] one of Mary Lavin's outstanding stories, is concerned with the nature of motherhood, husband-wife relationships, the failure of communication between intimately linked human beings, the true nature of love, as well as with the religious vocation, and it can therefore be read at many levels.

The social aspect of her daughter's vocation is uppermost in Mrs Latimer's mind and the exaggeration of this aspect marks Mary Lavin's criticism of it and of the attention paid to outward observances in religion. The following passage is taken from the most recently published version of the story:

Mrs. Latimer. Mrs. Latimer. Her Christian name

would probably be dropped — fall out of use —
become forgotten. Even Luke might, in time, feel
Meg too frivolous a name to call her except perhaps
when they were alone. Once already today — talking
to Reverend Mother — he had — to her astonishment — called her Margaret. She would become a
sort of exhibit. Would she perhaps be obliged to
assume an attitude? Expected to dress differently?
More discreetly? To give up smoking? In public
anyway! To put up holy pictures even in her
downstairs rooms? and what else? Oh yes! to punc-
tuate her conversation ·with pious little tags like
God willing, Thanks be to God and *God between
us and all harm.*

The physical sacrifice involved also occurs to Mrs
Latimer. She thinks it must be regarded differently by
men and women for Luke finds chastity 'unnatural,
abnormal, abhorrent', whereas she thinks women have
'a curious streak of chastity in them no matter how long
they had been married or how ardently they had loved',
so she is not worried by her daughter sacrificing the
blessings of marriage and motherhood. She is shown as
confusing in her mind the meanings of chastity and
prudery, sexual purity and sexual repression, and she
has always been too embarrassed to tell her daughter
about sex.

The spiritual advantages of having a daughter to pray
for her Mrs Latimer treats very lightly. She does not
believe God has chosen Angela, 'Angela had taken it
into her head and gone'.

Even though evidently enjoying sex herself, with no
evidence of the streak of chastity she has ascribed to all
women, Mrs Latimer is prudish about contemplating
her own sex life, in case she falls into evil thoughts.
She thinks: 'Angela was going to miss it all . . . . Her
mind rambled back over the past — and indeed the

not-so distant past — and she thought about the bliss —
oh the bliss of — but better not to think about such
things, especially of the nights when they were first
married and young and inexperienced and when — No.
No. She must stamp out those thoughts. She must
suppress those blissful memories'. She must persuade
herself that God has called their child to 'Higher Things'
but her real opinion is: 'The Church had the trump card
when it came to talking about love. The fulfilling of the
law. Greater love hath no man! All that bosh'.

Love for Mrs Latimer remains at a strictly earthy,
phallic level. Thinking how she might have explained to
Angela the kind of love she will give up, she asks herself:
'What would she have said then? Not that love was
noble. Not that it was kind. Generous? No. Gentle?
No. Dignified? (That was laughable!) In short, love was
nothing that could be described in a way that would
have an appeal for an idealistic young girl whose head
was full of poetry. Why even the poets themselves
hadn't been able to describe it. *There had fallen a
splendid tear from the passion tree at the gate.* Lines
like that might convey something to one when one was
a bit older and understood the underlying sugges-
tions . . .'

The irony is here directed against Mrs Latimer's
superficial understanding, her refusal to face facts. It is
she herself who is retreating into an unreal role as the
Nun's Mother and failing to communicate with her
daughter at a crucial point in the child's life. When the
episode of the man exposing himself under the lamppost
is narrated at the end of the story Mrs Latimer has a
vision of the same man reaching out with sweaty, fat
fingers towards Angela, who has become a water lily.
Angela is cool and inaccessible looking. Has she ever
been kissed?

Angela's previous apparent impatience about going
to mass had hardly led her parents to suppose she had a

vocation. Has she then entered the convent as an escape from sex after being disgusted by the pervert? Or has Mrs Latimer, with her incomprehension of the religious vocation, and any degree of love beyond that related to human sexuality, failed to understand her daughter's true calling? The church's understanding of 'greater love hath no man' is as far from Mrs Latimer's 'all that bosh' as her bliss with Luke is from the exposed penis under the lamppost.

In 'Chamois Gloves' the social dimension of the religious vocation is again ridiculed. In this story three postulants are about to take their first vows, an important social occasion before which reverend mother fusses about the lack of proper grapefruit spoons.

The heroine of the story is Veronica, youngest of the postulants, who has been continuously happy since she joined the novitiate, and is worried because 'where was the sacrifice if there was no pain of loss, no anguish of indecision?'

Veronica's sister Mabel comes to the ceremony. She has just given birth to her first child. Veronica does not want to know the details: 'She didn't want to be priggish but if God ordained that certain things were to be outside her experience, she didn't care to know anything about them'. After the ceremony is over and the relatives have left, Veronica feels depressed. The narrator here introduces a jocular note, the effect of which is to stress the young nun's childishness. 'Fatigue had brought a certain dejection, and her shoulders drooped slightly. And could she but have seen it, beside her, the feathered wings of her guardian angel drooped still more.' While washing out the chamois gloves left behind by Mabel, the slimy feeling of the wet skin reminds Veronica of past memories. Her sacrifice now strikes her for the first time and she weeps, at which the guardian angel, 'cupping two tears in her hand' sped for Heaven.

This whimsical treatment of a young girl's vocation never mentions any aspect of spiritual love, and we get the impression that Veronica, like Angela, is too immature to realise what she is undertaking. A religious vocation is, after all, not just giving up sex, feminine accoutrements and the joys of motherhood, but also gaining something in their place supposedly worth much more.

In the third story, 'My Vocation', the ironic treatment of the wrong reasons for having a vocation becomes comedy of the melodramatic kind rarely attempted by Mary Lavin. The flippant and mischievous first person narrator, recounts how she once answered an advertisement for Mission Postulants. She comes from a poor Dublin family and would normally only expect to become a lay sister because most Orders demand a dowry. This young girl enters into the whole thing as a joke. Her friend Sis points out that the only Orders with no lay sisters are the Little Sisters of the Poor and the Visiting Sisters. For such nuns, with no social pretensions, the family expecting a visit would never rush round borrowing all their neighbours' best bits of furniture in order to impress. When the Mission nuns arrive, however, they do not notice the grand display for their benefit, behave in a patronising way and only ask the girl if her hair is clean (i.e. lice-free). Beneath this comic story there is underlying criticism of the worldly aspects of religious orders and the wrong reasons for which girls often join them.

Mary Lavin's most recent story about a nun is 'Eterna', which also contains ironic comment on the anti-intellectual trends in contemporary Irish society. The Eterna in the story is a novice and artist who falls off a ladder while painting a replica of Our Lady of Good Counsel on the walls of the chapel, and cuts her arm. The young doctor called in to treat her has intellectual tastes and finds the district a cultural desert.

The nun, outwardly meek, conveys to him an air of 'unspeakable arrogance'. This, with her artistic talents and youth, intrigues him and during subsequent visits to treat her he becomes friendly. He asks her why she has chosen to shut herself up in a convent. Her reply is:

> A fat lot I'd have seen of God's creation . . . . I was born in this town. The oldest of ten! But for the nuns, I'd never have got anything more than elementary schooling. They educated me for nothing! And it was they who taught me to draw and to paint. There was a nun who had done her novitiate in Louvain, and she taught me all I know.

The Order had accepted her without a dowry because of her talent but she has never been to a good art gallery. In a wastepaper basket she finds an old National Gallery catalogue which she shows the doctor, 'clasping it to her bosom with all the ardour of a saint at the stake clasping a crucifix'. Carried away by her enthusiasm the doctor shows Eterna that he is attracted to her. At once he feels appalled at his breach of professional ethics, 'and from her stare he knew that to her he was some slimy, toadlike thing that had crawled out of a painting of Bosch's "Temptation of St. Anthony".'

It is evident that Eterna's religious vocation is inextricably interwoven with her love of art — art and God to her are one. Eterna later leaves the convent and the story is based on a flashback starting from when the doctor, now middle-aged and married to prosaic Annie, thinks he sees a crazy woman who looks like Eterna wandering round the National Gallery. But he tells himself:

> Why should he care even if it was Eterna? If she's

gone a bit cracked, what about it? As Annie would
say, she was probably headed that way from the start.
People had to learn to clip their wings if they wanted
to survive in this world. They had to keep their
feet on the ground. That was what Annie had taught
him to do — God bless her.

This cleverly developed story awakens issues far beyond
that of a religious vocation and takes the whole concept
of religious vocation outside the convent walls. It shows
once again that many, perhaps most, religious vows are
taken for the wrong reasons; that a vocation can be as
easily fulfilled by a lay doctor as by a nun, for it should
be based not on a circumscribed life pattern but on a
particular state of mind. The stifling of the true springs
of Christianity by prescriptive dogma is the equivalent
of the stifling of imaginative joy by material care. The
doctor retreats into the National Gallery from his wife,
busy at the sales, just as the nun retreats from her
family into the convent. This dichotomy of the material
and the spiritual is a continuing one and the only question is how much should the wings be clipped before
one becomes completely earth-bound? And once
clipped do they ever grow again?

As well as criticising the wrong reasons for adopting
the religious calling, Mary Lavin also shows admiration
for those who accept and fulfil this extremely demanding role. Both criticism of, and admiration for priests
appear in her work.

In the minds of some Irish people still today the
priest is the Church, and in the minds of some priests
there used to be — though this is passing — a tendency
to confuse devotion to the Church with devotion to
themselves. Long after historic reasons for putting the
priest in a special category had disappeared, the his-
torically conditioned emotional response remained in
Ireland, as Sean Ó Faoláin points out:

The Church in Ireland is a victim of one of the most influential facts in our history, namely that the Reformation in England coincided with the Conquest in Ireland. The result is that when we lost our native aristocracy after the Williamite wars (1691), but still held firmly to our traditional faith, we were left with a purely popular or peasant church, much too poor and too harassed to develop an intellectual life either among its priests or its people. In the circumstances the Church, not unnaturally, found it easier to rule by command rather than by advice or persuasion. It is still locked in that imperious tradition, unable or unwilling to admit that its flock has been developing ahead of it.[8]

Socially the priest is still of first importance in small towns, and the leader of his flock — like 'The Pastor of Six Mile Bush'. This is a remote Galway parish, to which three students walk because two of them have made disparaging remarks about the priesthood, and the particular pastor of this parish, which the third, who is a seminarian, refuses to believe. Though the story is at the most obvious level a moral tale about not listening to scandalous talk, and the priest emerges vindicated from all suspicion of gluttony or worse, the final impression of this story is ambivalent because of the clusters of images Mary Lavin casts, as it were, in the reader's path. The setting of the story and the type-cast priest who is never named, creates an allegorical vignette from which wider moral implications of spiritual aridity emerge. As the young men walk through the desolate bog:

By moonlight, strange effects were created in this flat slatey country: the white medals of lichen glared garishly here and there, and when a shrill bird of prey passed over the road between the earth and the moon, the eye was taken less by the real bird, than it was by its great shadow that skimmed on the ground beneath it.

The priest's house eventually emerges. Lit by the moon it looks like a stage set. The other props highlighted round the house are sheep, a crop of pale green wheat, a graveyard with some crosses in granite and the bleached bones of a sheep's head.

The priest's dining room they peer into is depressing with black, lichenous deposit on the faded red wallpaper, yellow patches of damp, crumbling cornices and falling plaster. The old priest, yellow-skinned and skull-like with age, eats mutton and rather improbably hands mutton out through the window to his starving parishioners who consume it seated on tombstones. This pastor-shepherd of his people-flock lives off the sheep who graze round his house, and also off the sheeplike people whose contributions buy him his food. He models his own life on the Lamb of God whose sacrificial death he celebrates with each mass he offers.

The wheatfield, symbolising the bread of life, is the only emblem of fertility in the story, and the noise of the ears brushing against the hands of the young men makes a sibilant sound in the still night as they retreat across the bog.

This fantastically eerie story leaves an impression of torpor. It is a vision of spiritual hopelessness. Robert Caswell has pointed out the significance of the three names given the students,[9] but the spiritual rebirth Caswell sees present in the minds of the three young men through their 'baptism of experience' in the story, seems an inadequate explanation, for surely the full allegorical impact of the story shows that this priest, leader of his people, is doing nothing to alleviate their physical or spiritual poverty. He feeds them but does not encourage them to feed themselves. His way of life hardly gives an encouraging picture of their future vocations to the seminarist (keeper of souls) or the two medical students (keepers of bodies), however blameless it may be in an ethical sense.

The sense of self-importance encouraged in some priests by the laity emerges in stories such as 'A Wet Day', 'A Pure Accident' and 'The Shrine'; but Mary Lavin also gives us a humble and kindly priest in Father Hugh of the late stories 'Happiness' and 'The Lost Child'.

Her priests are shown failing to rise above the very human weaknesses attendant upon their calling. They may be obsessed by their church building programme; by the evils of sin particularly as expressed through sex; more concerned with ugliness than beauty, with moral superstition than the joys of life. Chastity not charity occupies the front of their minds more often than not.

Mary Lavin judges a priest first as a man. 'A Wet Day' contains an ironic sketch of a self-centred cleric. The narrator is a young student staying with her aunt whose views are those of the author herself in 1944. The aunt 'was beginning to realise that in my estimate of a man's worth I did not allow much credit for his cloth'. The aunt, however, lives in mortal fear of offending the old parish priest. Yet, conscious as this priest is of his poor diet and damp church, like the Levi in the tale of the Good Samaritan, he shows scant sympathy for his niece and her young fiancé when the latter is taken seriously ill in his house. Even though the niece, who visits him regularly, is a good cook and a trained nurse, he pretends he has no thermometer and sends the sick man back to Dublin where he dies a few days later. The priest, terrified of death, is filled with the studied self-regard of old age — a common enough failing after all.

'A Pure Accident' which has a strong plot and clever alternation of comedy and tragedy, is also about lack of

charity, here taken to greater depths. The canon in this
story is authoritative and domineering. He laughs at his
own jokes and makes fun of others, assured of his own
superiority. He has built up a wall of status round himself to compensate for life's handicaps. The story turns
on his refusal to allow extra light to be put in the
dark porch of the church. The poor box has been rifled,
and Father Patton has been sent to hide in the porch
and catch the thief.

One of the three laymen in the story, Andy Devine,
has an older sister who reared him after his mother died
but now lives alone. On their way home the three men
pass Annie paying her evening visit to the Church.
As she enters the dark porch she collides with the
large Father Patton, falls and breaks her leg, though in
the dark the men do not realise this. The priest and the
three men bundle her into the back of a car and take her
home but find she has lost her doorkey. Father Patton,
afraid of the canon, thinks only of getting rid of Annie
at Andy's house and pays no attention to her moans of
pain. Eventually they discover her thigh bone sticking
out of her leg.

In hospital Annie can only think of who will foot the
bill. She waits in vain for Father Patton's visit. When
he comes at last he makes it clear that the church will
not pay, for he fears to tell the canon. Father Patton
knows his only chance of getting his own parish and
escaping from the canon is to keep in the bishop's
good books.

Some of the stresses behind the priestly vocation
emerge in this story as Father Patton recounts how he
had a nervous breakdown in the seminary, and we see
that the canon's assessment of him is correct; his mother
forced him to go through with his ordination. He both
fears and hates the unsympathetic canon, and he bursts
into tears of self-pity. All this priest's illusions and
neurotic fears are revealed to the partially comprehend-

ing Annie and we see that emotionally he is terribly stunted and ignorant. Is this necessarily one of the sacrifices a man must make in exchange for Holy Orders?

We can only feel pity for this man, victim of a rigorous conditioning he is quite incapable of overcoming, and which his faith has failed to sublimate. He leaves Annie thinking that his life has been all in boxes, the boxlike seminary, confession boxes, poor boxes, collection boxes and pamphlet boxes. 'Even God was kept in a box, shut up and locked into one. What else was the Tabernacle but only a box?' Reading such a passage it is evident that the author feels strongly about the limitations of celibacy.

'The Shrine', one of Mary Lavin's most recent stories, contains criticism of religious shrines standing in the way of possible industrial development of which Ireland has such need. This story illustrates the influence of the catholic church in Ireland on social development, all the more effectively because this canon is a sympathetic and well-defined character.

'The Shrine' in question, according to Mary Lavin, refers to Knock, County Mayo.[10] The fictionalised canon is the uncle and guardian of the narrator Mary. As her mother died when she was small she has spent her school holidays with the canon who has become a father figure in her life, and they know each other intimately. The canon is not emotionally stultified and his love and generosity to his niece have helped channel thwarted emotions he might otherwise have repressed. He is, however, a priest first, a man of strict principles and convictions and, like most of Mary Lavin's priests, sins of the flesh rank with him uppermost.

The canon's ideas conflict with those of Don, a geologist and Mary's fiancé, who claims that the development of mineral wealth would be much more beneficial to the region than the shrine. Mary supports

Don's argument, in spite of her affection for her uncle: 'Could there be any real possibility that the impoverished earth out there could be made to yield a better livelihood for the people and free them from ignominiously selling cheap religious objects to the sick and dying?' Whereas the canon believes that: 'Our little Shrine is bringing more prosperity to the people hereabouts with every year that passes. It's not only providing them with their daily bread but giving them spiritual food as well'. Mary cannot understand how an intelligent and sensitive man, such as her uncle, who reads several languages and appreciates art, can suffer from such a delusion.

For the canon, however, the spiritual comes first and to him the shrine is an outward expression of this. His personal ambition and emotions are also centred round this physical spot. Mary analyses his trouble: '. . . it was love, or lack of it, that was at the root of all the contradictions on it. He thought he'd cut out all need for it from his body and although for a time his natural feelings for his sister, and later for herself, seemed to fill the vacancy, it was not enough. The vacuum had to be filled and he's filled it with devotion to the Shrine'. The canon voices the strength of the church power over Irish society when he tells Mary about Don's ideas:

'Whatever that fool of a fellow may have in mind, he doesn't know that backing is needed for every scheme whether it's sound or not. Not only here but in every country in the world. I can assure you that in holy Ireland there wouldn't be one solitary soul who'd back up any scheme that would', he paused, 'interfere with a place sanctified by tradition, and already hallowed by the presence of so many sick and suffering human beings!'

At the end of the story his love for Mary, smothered

anyway by the fear of scandal when he goes out with her in public, is overcome by annoyance at Don's potential rivalry. He telephones a contact in Dublin to make sure Don will not be offered the vacant district engineer's job.

Mary Lavin's most sympathetic priest characters are Father Tom, who appears in 'Villa Violetta' and Father Hugh of 'Happiness' and 'The Lost Child'. Father Tom brings a coach party of London-Irish travellers from Camden Town on a tour through Italy. He meets the widow Vera Traske and her young daughters in the Villa Violetta, Florence, a pension run by Irish nuns. Father Tom is sophisticated, balanced and warm-hearted with a strong personality. He confides to Vera that, once a banker, he had a late vocation after his fiancée was killed. He says: 'People don't realise it, but as we priests get older, it is the loss of paternity that is the hardest part of celibacy'. He now fills his life with the love he lavishes on his parishioners.

The Father Hugh in 'Happiness' and 'The Lost Child' is also a paternal character. In 'Happiness' he is close friend and surrogate father to the widow Vera Traske, who dies at the end of the story, and her three daughters. There is an autobiographical element in this character corresponding to personal circumstances in the author's own life. The family behave in Father Hugh's presence much as they would with a male member of the family. One daughter says: 'I'm so glad he *has* Mother, as well as her having him, because it must be awful the way most women treat them — priests, I mean — as if they were pariahs. Mother treats him like a human being — that's all!' And when it came to the widow's ears that there had been gossip about her and Father Hugh she says in astonishment, 'But he's only a priest!' The importance of love in the burgeoning of the full human being is stressed in the religious, as in the laity, throughout Mary Lavin's work.

In 'The Lost Child' more controversial aspects of religious opinion arise. This fifty-page story tells how Renée is received into the catholic church by Father Hugh in the presence of her husband Mike, a catholic, their two children and her sister Iris. There is irony in Renée's thoughts just after the ceremony. She thinks how she resisted conversion before marriage, yet now she accepts it willingly. In Ireland mixed marriages are celebrated in the sacristy or a side chapel, and Renée's mother had made difficulties over this. The unmarried sister Iris has reacted against her mother's attitude to marriage and has decided that marriage for the sake of it, is wrong. The old stresses and strains of a catholic-protestant prejudice are interwoven in this story with the theme of love in marriage, commented on by Iris, the single questioning woman who has maintained her economic and emotional independence and yet missed something — what?

Mike and Renée's marriage is fused by mutual self-interest and their responsibility for creating a family, but a deeply intimate understanding of, and support for each other also emerges when they are in trouble. This story also illustrates modern woman's developing sense of her own identity. Renée's power is vicarious but she asserts her independent ideas. She still lacks confidence and allows emotions to oversway reason. She is erratic, confused and often illogical, in spite of her university degree and ability to teach herself so much. She is shown to be more energetic, decisive and clear thinking when she acts alone, for she is emotionally dependent on Mike. Iris, much more logical than her sister, cannot swallow some of the catholic customs such as that which forbids the burying of unbaptised babies in consecrated ground. After Renée has had a miscarriage she starts worrying about the possible soul of her aborted foetus, and the church's teaching on this point makes her doubt her newly acquired loyalties. Iris then says: 'You can see why I didn't want you to rush into a religion that makes everything so hard — so *impossibly* hard'. To Iris faith and dogma are laudably distinct.

Mary Lavin would seem to suggest that the catholic church now desperately needs priests of Father Hugh's type. He can look a young woman deep in the eyes without embarrassment and is willing to doubt and question. His remark: 'You're a man after my own heart, Iris', points to his admission that women may after all be able to think and argue, though neither he nor Iris have got beyond the point of finding such a remark amusing. Some women, like Iris, prefer to stand on their own feet. Others, like Renée, need support and there is some suggestion in this story that the church is at present too much of a prop, does not yet treat the laity in a sufficiently adult way.

Renée is surprised, when Father Hugh instructs her, how unwilling he is to receive her into the church at all. Male dominance in relation to the religious life emerges from Renée's musing about the priest. 'It was just that, like his Church, he believed so staunchly in male superiority, he could not concede the possibility of the woman having the stronger pull in matters of the mind. And yet, in the end, it was the maleness of the Church that had, as Mike put it, hooked her. She could lean on it.'

This is a very modern story, outspoken and dense in meaning, showing a transitional society in which questioning of male and female roles, the structure and teachings of the church, conception and childbirth related to the birth of the soul and the body, are all inter-related and are in need of re-definition and discussion.

The story contains a clever description of Renée's feelings after the miscarriage, as she lies in a weak, semiconscious state. She worries lest one of the clots from her body contained her putative baby's soul. Father Hugh assures her: 'the Vatican may be prepared to admit to error in its theories of Limbo — it was never a dogma, you know'. This is an ironic comment on the impossible confusion in most people's minds between faith and all its trimmings, but shows hopeful progression from the catholic attitudes illustrated in the earlier story 'Limbo'.

An important channel for religious expression in Mary Lavin's work is her preoccupation with the theme of death.[11]

The catholic church's preoccupation with the 'saving of souls' relates life on earth to a preparatory stage on the road to eternity. The dead, from saints to sinners, form an integral body and therefore Holy Ireland is not just a few million living persons but an uncountable throng of souls, for whom the living feel kinship and whose influence may still be felt. As the narrator says in 'The Mouse': 'The dead are only really dead when they are no longer remembered by the living'. In 'Sunday brings Sunday' the priest prays for the dead at the end of mass in the words of the *De Profundis*. The sociological implications of such a tradition in a religiously committed society are, of course, immense. Already mentioned in this chapter are some of the impressions left on the childish mind as recorded by writers such as Edna O'Brien, James Joyce and Sean Ó Faoláin. Lavin stories 'The Dead Soldier', 'The Green Grave and the Black Grave', 'Bridal Sheets', 'A Happy Death', 'The Cemetery in the Demesne', 'The Will', 'Loving Memory', 'The Living' and many more, deal with different aspects of death, seriously or ironically, and an analysis of her stories reveals that in over half of them death is introduced in one form or another.

We here encounter, however, another level of what might be termed Mary Lavin's moral assumptions. For when she criticises religious proscription, or the moral

integrity of a person claiming to have a religious vocation, it is with the assumption that her readers will be
either sympathetic or antipathetic to her viewpoint;
whereas much, though not of course all, of her preoccupation with the theme of death is based on assumptions rooted in her own sociological background, and
this conditioning is, with her as with all of us, largely
unconscious, forming part of her own individual
concept of reality.

It is here necessary for the reader to make a projection of the imagination, particularly if the catholic, or
indeed Christian, background is strange to him, and to
ponder how Christian imagery may permeate, or at least
influence, the minds of Irish catholic writers. Paramount
among such imagery is that of the cross. This image is
itself an ambiguous one, incorporating as it does both
death and immortality, love and destruction, loss and
gain, hideous suffering and beatific triumph.

In the Celtic cross the circle round the cross-bar
could be said to represent both the crown of thorns and
the laurel wreath of the victor, or alpha/omega, the
circle of perpetuity.[12]

After the Reformation the crucifix, removed by the
protestant cult, became the focal point of catholic rites.
It was an object easily carried in his pocket by the
persecuted catholic priest which, set up with candles on
any table, converted it into an altar. Persecuted Irish
catholicism took refuge in the cross and the penitential
elements of Christianity.[13] The impression of this is
all-pervasive; those souls massacred by Cromwell, lost
in the Famine, killed in the Civil War and whose lives
still dribble out in acts of terrorism — their litany of
sacrifice is early impressed on a school child's mind,
parallel with the expiatory aspect of his religion. The
sign of the cross, kissing the crucifix on the Rosary,
the huge crucifix with a naked figure often marked with
drops of blood hanging over every altar — all this is far

more pervasive imagery than that of Christ's resurrection and hope. Christ is the suffering servant who was persecuted and won in the end, but at what a price.

Austin Clarke perhaps summed up the attitude of mind taken by many Irish poets, however different their methods of expression,[14] when he wrote in his two-line poem 'The Thorn':

> In your decline, when truth is bare,
> The thorn is seen without its crown.

This attitude, though dominant in Ireland, is not peculiarly Irish, as Teilhard de Chardin once pointed out.[15]

Today the conventional crucifix, merely as an image of suffering, no longer has the same impact on a society continually bombarded, through the mass media, with horror and violence, reading of tortures with no detail spared.[16] The penitential aspect of Christianity, which Irishmen have always sought escape from in drink, dancing and other so-called pagan activities, is antipathetic to the positive-thinking, younger generation of catholics, as we see in Mary Lavin's 'The Shrine'. The danger is that they may react by over-stressing the importance of the physical and the material which is just as bad. Mary Lavin, subject to her own conditioning, is drawn at the subconscious level to emblems of death and at the conscious level to the full recognition of the mystery of death, as a counterweight to the material, and because death can have a dual image representing both the summit of love and the epitome of destruction. She is simultaneously attracted by death and repelled by its tendency to dominate and depress life.

The priests and nuns in Mary Lavin's stories reflect her own ambivalent attitude, and are subject to the same limitations as other characters in her work. They are ironically treated for their failure to love, for their preoccupation with the material to the exclusion of the spiritual. They are heavily conditioned by habits of thought and reaction in various ways which impede the development of a true religious vocation — her Father Hugh being an exception. The celibate state as such is not criticised for causing emotional aridity — for the same attitude of mind is also found in some of her married characters, as it threatens widows and single women — but it is implied that an individual, for full emotional development, needs the opportunity to express truly intimate affection. Few are capable of sublimating all physical expression of love and expanding themselves to the full on a purely spiritual plane.

* * *

The ironic implications of Mary Lavin's work, considered in these three chapters can now be seen to be inter-related aspects of her over-riding social concern. Her irony originates at two levels. Her irony of provocation masks the moralist. She dislikes hypocrisy, whether expressed in terms of social conformity, pious practice, or self-righteousness. Ironically treated characters wrap themselves in a blanket of pretence, at best acting out of habit because they have not thought out the reasons for their behaviour, or at worse deliberately using a social framework such as the class structure, marriage or the religious vocation to give themselves a sense of status or social support. By revealing the ridiculous aspect of such behaviour Mary Lavin hopes to provoke a greater self-consciousness and an awareness in her readers of the shortcomings of their society.

Alongside this irony of provocation can be discerned Mary Lavin the idealist, who uses irony to conceal her personal disillusionment. Her attention to the intuitive, the spiritual dimension, the importance of love, are all part of her ideal. Mary Lavin has said:

I think every moment of life creates its own moral decision, and each time a proper moral solution must be found . . . . How can you say who is a committed Christian? For myself, I would try to sacrifice the material to the spiritual. I hope I would succeed.[17]

But, surrounded by practical necessity, ideological habit and social pressures to conform, to live in this way is a perpetual struggle.

Fundamentally irony springs from the knowledge that comedy and tragedy emanate from the same source — and it is supposedly an Irish characteristic to be sharply aware of these closely linked opposites. It is less typical, however, for modern Irish writers to use irony in Mary Lavin's gentle, even sly, way.

Wayne C. Booth has pointed out that the recognition of irony depends on an unmistakable conflict between beliefs expressed and the beliefs we hold, and suspect the author of holding (*The Rhetoric of Irony*, Chicago 1974). Irony reflects personal as well as cultural ambiguities. At first a reader may not recognise all the ironic implication, and his understanding of this will deepen the more he reads the author in question, and the more he knows about the author's particular social circumstances and environment. This is an intricate process, even with regard to a contemporary writer, and in Mary Lavin's case her Irish world has changed a great deal, and herself with it, since the 1940s when she first started to write.

Finding in her own life how hard it is to maintain a balance between dependence and independence, hard-headed reality and fantasy, between order and chaos, love and habit, revolt and acceptance, restraint and excess, Mary Lavin has chosen the path of rebuke not rebellion, the wry smile not the bitter outburst. This does not mean, however, that her feelings are any the less pronounced. She does not flood the reader with emotion-charged value judgments. Her aim is to prod not shock, and she allows the reader to construct for himself the interpretation he wishes to put on her work. The exact reaction will depend on an individual reader's level of awareness, past experience, and the degree of existential difference between his and Mary Lavin's world.

4 Artistic Intentions

Feeling, or looking more closely than normal into the human heart, was from the first Mary Lavin's ground theme. Her ways of doing so progress, however, as she herself develops as a person.

Her first volume of short stories, *Tales from Bective Bridge,* contains the Synge-like 'The Green Grave and the Black Grave', which contrasts with the Joycean echoes to be found in 'At Sallygap'. As a young writer she already showed herself most at home in domestic interior stories of feeling such as 'Love is for Lovers' or 'Lilacs'.

Explicit indications of Mary Lavin's artistic intentions are contained in the techniques she employs in two early stories, 'A Story with a Pattern' (written in 1939, published 1946) and 'The Widow's Son' (written earlier but first published 1951). Both stories experiment with narrative method, and both illustrate their author's abiding refusal to limit the nature of reality to what is seen, known as fact, or believed to be true.

In 'A Story with a Pattern' the first person author/ narrator is at a cocktail party, when another guest comes up. He criticises her work, gives her advice about it and then tells her what he calls one of his father's 'real, true stories'. The faults of this half-educated man, as seen by the twenty-seven-year-old author, are the dangers she herself is alert to. She decides this man is dogmatic, over-explicit and didactic. He says her stories lack substance or plot; they appeal only to women. She replies: 'Life has very little plot'. The man in this story anticipates future criticism of her work. He likes fiction to be a distraction from reality and impose some arbitrary selection of events to give everyday life a semblance of significance. Mary Lavin's way is to concentrate not on events but on feelings. As a young writer she has already decided on her method. She does not care whether her stories only appeal to women, or not. She intends her work to lack shape, plot or pattern.

Her middle-aged interlocutor in this story explains: 'There may be times when life seems formless, and when our actions seem to be totally unrelated to each other, but for that again there are thousands of times when incidents in life not only show a pattern, but a pattern as clear and well-marked as the pattern on this carpet!'

Mary Lavin wrote stories with patterns at the beginning of her career, two such being 'The Green Grave and the Black Grave' and 'At Sallygap', but she always prefers to subordinate action plot to the contingency of feeling. In 'A Story with a Pattern' she stands back as author/narrator and listens to her character introducing his father's true story, noticing the difference of narrative tone, conveying feeling, which creeps into his voice:

I think my main reason for encouraging him to go on was that I wanted to hear how he would tell it. For, since the time he first came over to me with such a sophisticated manner, a change had taken place in both his manner and his voice, and even in his very vocabulary. With his first words about Murty

Lockhart the emphasis he had been laying on every second word disappeared altogether and he became instead, unsure, halting and inclined to look at me questioningly in between every sentence. And when he was speaking a short time, I noticed with interest that it was not his voice at all I was listening to, but the voice of his father who had told the story to him. His memory had stored not only the incidents of that story but the very words in which it had been told, and the very voice of the man who first strung them together. It was the voice of an aged and credulous man telling an incredible story with a kind of fright at its seeming purpose.

The narrator of the Murty Lockhart tale within a tale is given to digression and inconsequentiality. He is so eager to tell his story that he fails to bring any character to life, and there are errors in his point of view. A further ironic fold is added to the story as the reader realises he is not simply listening to a man repeating his father's story, but to a man retelling a story with his own interpretations and embroideries of fact, for this must be so with all stories. The strong plotline and coincidental ending are those of someone who, like Murty, finds faith a poor substitute for proof, and who when he must have faith likes to feel there is a *deus ex machina* controlling destiny.

This clever story with a pattern, narrated within a story without a pattern, makes it clear that much as Mary Lavin may enjoy listening to the spellbinding effect of strong plot-line tales it is not a genre she herself wishes to write more than occasionally. As she later stated in her critical Preface, stories for her are 'the vagaries and contrarieties' of the human heart which have their own integral design, their own reality. It is this design which superimposes itself on any plot a story may accidentally contain. When she occasionally allows plot to dominate and create a neat ending, as in 'Villa Violetta', the story collapses into sentimentality.

That feeling outstrips plot is also revealed in 'The Widow's Son'. The author tells us at once this is an essay in fiction, a story with two endings. The first ending tells how Packy rides full tilt on his bicycle down the hill, jams on his brakes to avoid a hen, is thrown off and killed. His mother asks: 'Why did he put the price of an old clucking hen above the price of his own life?'

The author intervenes before the introduction of the second ending:

> . . . it is sometimes easier to invent than to remember accurately, and were this not so two great branches of creative art would wither in an hour: the art of the story-teller, and the art of the gossip. So, perhaps, if I try to tell you what I myself think might have happened had Packy killed that cackling old hen, you will not accuse me of abusing my privileges as a writer. After all, what I am about to tell you is no more of a fiction than what I have already told, and I lean no heavier now upon your credulity than, with your full consent, I did in the first instance.

For the second ending Packy descends the hill, fails to brake in time, kills the hen and runs back to look at it. The furious widow picks up the hen's corpse and belabours her son with it. She scolds Packy in front of listening neighbours. He explains he rode so fast to tell her he had won a scholarship, but the widow is afraid to show her joyful pride and shames Packy before the village. That night he runs away to sea. The widow's pride in her son has caused him to forfeit his scholarship.

The author ends: 'Perhaps all our actions have this double quality about them; this possibility of alternative, and thus it is only by careful watching, and absolute sincerity, that we follow the path that is destined for us, and, no matter how tragic that may be, it is better than the tragedy we bring upon ourselves'. A writer can manipulate plot. It is his responsibility to reveal feeling and behaviour, but the reader's to pick up the tone and work out the implications. Why — Mary Lavin is asking the reader to explain — did the widow get into far more of a state over the death of the hen than she did over the death of her son?

One of Mary Lavin's admired authors, George Sand, wrote her pastoral romances inspired by an allegorical Holbein engraving which shows a bowed and ragged labourer ploughing, accompanied by the frisky skeleton of death armed with a whip. She said of the simple peasant about whom she wrote:

> *Eh bien, tel qu'il est, incomplet et condemné à une eternelle enfance, il est encore plus beau que celui chez qui la science a etouffé le sentiment.*[1]
> (Ah well, just as he is, incomplete and condemned to eternal childishness, he is still worthier than one in whom knowledge has stifled feeling.)

One reason Mary Lavin so often writes about the past, about simple people and small events, is because she hopes thus to find it easier to write stories of feeling, set in societies where action and ambition are more limited, where knowledge has not stifled feeling, and where the dramatic context of a person's life more often centres in emotion and memory.

'The Green Grave and the Black Grave' is a story about such characters, and like much of Mary Lavin's earlier work it is full of slow, repetitive phrases which come well from the mouths of these peasant characters.

It is written almost entirely in a singing dialogue representing transposed Gaelic. The short narrative passages are rhythmical and alliterative, so that the whole, with its formulaic devices of incantatory repetition and dramatic anticipation, creates a marvellous tale for telling, rather than reading.

In this story a young fisherman from the western islands of Ireland is drowned at sea on a windless night. The mackerel fishermen who find the body know the widow, an inland woman, believes there is a curse on wives buried ashore whose husbands' drowned bodies have never been recovered. By the end of the story they realise, however, that the wife is drowned too.

These fishermen's perception of reality is the age-old one of man, before education sharpened his logical powers of analysis and atrophied his intuition. For them reality is incorporated in their observation of natural phenomena; the spirits of nature and the spirit of man are part of the same essential being and can react one on the other by their intrinsic vitality. To express this instinctive feeling of being interpenetrated, enveloped or permeated by nature they personify natural forces and confront them with the living force in humans:

On a fine night the women lie down to sleep, and if any woman has a power over the sea, with her white feet in the water and her black hair in the wind and a bright fire in her heart, the sea can only wait until that woman's spirit is out of her body, likely back home in the inlands, and then the sea serpent gives a slow turn-over on his scales, one that you wouldn't heed to yourself, maybe, and you standing up with no hold on the oars; and before there's time for more than the first shout out of you the boat is logging-down to the depths of the water. And all the time the woman that would have saved you, with her willing and wishing for you, is in the deep bed of a dark sleep, having no knowledge of the thing that has happened until she hears the loud-handed knocking of the neighbour on the door outside.

The feel and look of the sea as spiky, spiteful, spittle, scabby, scurvy, forked and venomous, the sounds and colours of this story, are used to illustrate the men's vivid perceptions. The world for them is immediate; their concerns are actual; they have powerful memories; they accept death and the mysteries of natural phenomena. The sea is a serpent, the candleflame runs its hands over the door. Such physical reaction to sense impressions, such visual clarity of imagination, is for most modern adults only recaptured in dreams, or in dreamlike estates — hence the visionary imprint of this story, which Mary Lavin never subsequently recaptured with such intensity. This strong story of sea and shore, which takes place in subdued light, lit by glitter of fish scales, whiteness of breaking wave, shine of a dead man's eyes, silver-dripping oar and candle-flicker, seems kindred to some nether world, set apart from time or space.

'Bridal Sheets', another peasant story about a drowning in which the young inland widow survives her husband, was written twenty years later. What Brede really mourns is not her husband but her unworn trousseau. She is not keen to use her new embroidered sheets on his corpse. To her they are a symbol of sex, and for the public to gaze upon them is tantamount to indecent exposure. The ambiguity and distortion of feeling shown in this story is deliberately grotesque.[2]

Brede, unable to wear her smart clothing, has lost her sense of identity, as she has not yet become one of the islanders. In the same way Flora in 'The Becker Wives' does not succeed in identifying herself with the Beckers, another close-knit group. Flora, failing to recreate her new identity, eludes reality and assumes the identity of one of the group. Brede, the recent bride, clings to her sheets as part of the only identity she knows. Brede and Peigin, the two principal characters in 'Bridal Sheets', represent two Irelands, land and sea, bourgeois and peasant. The contrast in their feelings is exaggerated to stress the fact that what is real and important to one person may be unreal and of no importance to another. At what point incongruity enters such a situation depends on the social conditioning, or beliefs, of the individual.

But if feeling within the human heart is Mary Lavin's ground theme there are bound to be some who will find irksome not only her enlargement of the limits of acceptable reality, but also the narrow sphere she involves in the description of her chosen design. Her deliberate muting of the sexual response, so unusual in modern literature, will be faulted by some; others will criticise her refusal to enter the political arena. Her only political story, 'The Patriot Son', parodies patriotic heroism and provides what Frank O'Connor has called 'an irreverent footnote to Irish revolutionary literature'.

The reason why 'At Sallygap' stands out among Mary Lavin's earlier stories is that its action analyses a simple character trying to come to grips with his feelings. Manny appeals and enters the reader's imagination. No other character is as deeply studied until autobiographical work in the 1960s such as 'In a Café'. 'Lemonade', also of this period, shows Mary Lavin drawing upon memories of her childhood to create a firmly rooted beginning, to which she adds a loose and rambling fictional ending. The naive child's point of view is an unsure one, and the distancing of events further hinders the reader for the author has here neither committed herself wholeheartedly to autobiography nor to fiction. The mixture of personal memory and invention in 'Lemonade' creates a hybrid and flaccid reality.

The degree of self-awareness which characters portray is directly related to the development of the author's own confidence, maturity and sense of identity. Much of her earlier work writes out cast-off selves with which the weight of the past, hopes and fears, images of womanhood inherited from her parents, had swathed her.

Mary Lavin's early stories reveal, for the most part, a very narrow projection of reality. Apart from the simple fables she most often concentrated on one character, as in 'Miss Holland' and 'Brother Boniface', or the reactions between a pair of contrasting characters of the same sex, or a couple, as in 'Sunday brings Sunday', 'A Woman Friend', 'A Visit to the Cemetery', 'Love is for Lovers', 'The Inspector's Wife', and others. In her early volumes, however, she occasionally diverges from this narrow probe by setting up wider social echoes in the more richly nuanced stories such as 'The Becker Wives', 'A Happy Death', 'At Sallygap', or 'The Green Grave and the Black Grave'. The successful enlarging of her artistic probe inevitably incorporates flexible levels of reality, narrative tone suited to character, and greater creative daring.

As the promise of her best early stories, mentioned above, marks the first flowering of her artistic talent, so the publication of *The Great Wave* volume, and the variance within it, marks the first fruits of her maturity. The title story is based on a dramatically related flashback from the boyhood memory of the protagonist Jimeen, now a bishop. The great wave itself symbolises the force of visionary imagination controlled by credibility of plot. Mary Lavin here shows she *can* write dramatically, though she usually prefers not to do so. The wave is described thus:

It was as if the whole sea had been stood up on its

edge, like a plate on a dresser. And down that wall
of water there slid a multitude of dead fish.

And then, down the same terrible wall, sliding
like the dead fish, came an oar; a solitary oar. And a
moment afterwards, but inside the glass wall, imprisoned, like a glass dome, he saw — oh God! — a
face, looking out at him, staring out at him through
a foot of clear green water. And he saw it was the
face of Marteen. For a minute the eyes of the dead
man stared into his eyes.[3]

To Jimeen the memory of his childhood experience in
the great wave is real, and the telling of it appears real
to us. To the islanders, who have reinhabited the island
after the wave had swept all before it, this tragedy is
already historical legend, tinged with fantasy. Actuality
is continually in the process of being turned into
memory. How real is memory? The nature of reality
for each of us is based on the nature of our acquired and
inherited knowledge and beliefs. Jimeen is now a
learned bishop, yet while under the spell of this powerful memory imaginative feeling sweeps him out of the
present, even as the wave once swept him onto the cliff
top.

Credibility and memory emerge again as two themes
from *The Great Wave* volume which also contains
'Loving Memory', the last of the Grimes family stories,
and 'The Yellow Beret' about a Dublin couple who
suspect, but cannot quite believe, that their son is
involved in a murder.

There are also two first person narrated stories in
The Great Wave, 'The Mouse'[4] and 'My Molly', as well
as the 'I-protagonist' of 'The Living'. Mary Lavin
previously used the first person narrator in 'Say could
that lad be I?', 'A Story with a Pattern', 'The Small
Bequest' and the 'I-protagonist' in 'My Vocation' and a
recent autobiographical story 'Tom'. The first person

conversational narrator of 'My Molly' gives the story an additional oral intimacy and introduces shifting concepts of time which complicate interpretation for the reader.

The story is told by the husband/narrator. It is about the impossibility of fully understanding the feelings and motives of another, even a wife of ten years' standing whom you love and trust implicitly. Molly is inexplicably attached to old Sam, a saddler in the town who disappears after she has known him three months. She decides he has gone to Dublin and finds him there paddling on the end of the deepwater pier. She brings him back to live with her husband and children. The expedition to Dublin is recounted secondhand by the narrator from Molly's description of it, but the uncertain tone comes from the use of tenses in relation to the narrator's thoughts about his wife. He starts: 'What I couldn't understand was why my Molly took it so badly. We were only six months in the town at the time'. Describing his wife he passes into the present tense. 'Not that I understand her that well. All unexpected she is: my Molly. She's not a bit like what you'd think from looking at her.'

In the following excerpt the narrator withdraws from the present with each successive sentence, and he illustrates that ellipsis which so often occurs between feelings, thought and their expression in words:

> But I always feel that luck isn't something you get hanging on a bush — especially good luck. Some people attract it. Molly did. She had tact, too, Molly had — or so I was told. A funny kind of tact it seemed to me. I used to think tact meant always doing the right thing, but after living with Molly I began to think it was more like always doing the wrong thing and no harm coming out of it, but only good. Do you know what I mean?

With this rhetorical question the reader is invited to compare his experience with that of the narrator. Molly is both the perpetual wife, and the specific one. She has intuitions and feelings which her husband cannot fathom. The story reacts on the reader at two levels, first explicitly and secondly at the intuitive level of communication between the couple, beyond words and inexpressible in print. Present and past mingle in kaleidoscopic fashion, for this is a story about un-explained feeling, in which time takes second place.

Benedict Kiely said of Mary Lavin's early work that she erects brick by brick the House of Stolidity and then squeezes an imp through the keyhole.[5] The imp may be the tone of ironic criticism implying ridicule against stereotyped social responses, or it may, as here, be the imp of contingency about mutual, and often intuitive human comprehension, or the lack of it.

The uncertainty in the tone of the husband/narrator in 'My Molly' is based on his failure to understand his wife. The child first person narrator in 'The Living' fails to comprehend through immaturity. The same contingency of feeling is shown in many previous third person narrated stories, starting with 'Miss Holland', right through the stolidity of the Grimes family stories which end with Bedelia and Daniel's voyage to the United States. Uncertainty also appears as the quizzical self-mockery Mary Lavin has introduced into semi-autobiographical stories about widows Mary and Vera. Such uncertainty, in all its forms, represents a search for the meaning of life and a definition of personal identity. For Mary Lavin nothing is certain, and the nature of reality, like time itself, is in a continual state of flux.

With 'A Likely Story', written for children about young Packy's visit to the leprechauns, Mary Lavin tried showing reality in the guise of a fairy tale. Packy's mother never believes his stories, hence the equivocal title. Packy's prosaic thoughts, as voiced in the story, contrast with the fantastic situation in which he finds himself, amid golden harps and milk pails, being washed down by fairy women. Mary Lavin has in this tale returned momentarily to that country of the gods beyond logic, as James Stephens recommended.[6] She has written a number of stories about children but only two for child readers specifically, the other being 'The Second-Best Children of the World'. 'A Likely Story' will be enjoyed by adults who can still recall the luminous strength of their own childish imagination, for it represents a child's limited view of reality in which fact and fantasy are still fluid, feelings still immature.

States of feeling and the degree of self-awareness in characters are directly related in Lavin's work to her own concept that the multi-faced and ambiguous nature of reality depends entirely on the person through whom it is projected. Many of her simpler characters are shown through their feelings, represented by imagery which appeals to the visual, aural or olfactory sense, other than through intellectual effort or self-analysis. Awareness in other characters is limited by youth or lack of experience, as in 'A Cup of Tea', 'A Glimpse of Katey' or 'The Young Girls'. The growth of self-awareness may be stunted by a prescribed way of thinking, so often subject to Mary Lavin's irony, outside which characters are afraid to venture, or inside which they remain for safety. This is illustrated by the mother's interior monologues in 'The Nun's Mother', by Lally in 'The Will', or by the Grimes family characters in the Castlerampart stories. Some characters' awareness is circumscribed by their narrow personal experience. There are those who feel and think but are inarticulate like Brother Boniface; or characters who represent the separation of the thinking and feeling selves typified in the pairs of females found in stories such as 'The Lilacs'. In later stories about more highly evolved indivi-

duals there are those who can think but in whom knowledge has stifled feeling, such as James in 'A Memory';
or those who feel but are ignorant, like Miss Lomas in
'The Mock Auction'.

The lead character of 'Cuckoo-Spit' (1964) is mature
and self-aware. In this story the distancing of the past
has gone, so has the leisurely repetition of earlier work.
The narrative style now represents the fast tempo, the
busy impatience of the present. One is also conscious
that the author speaks through this widow. Because of
her personal development this woman's sensitivity and
preoccupations make it impossible for her to reflect the
crystalline simplicity of response shown by an earlier
widow such as Ros in 'The Lilacs'. This is conveyed by
the shifting narrative tones between that of the widow
alone, and that of the widow with Fergus, suggesting the
non-verbal communication passing between them.

It is through such apparent trivia that the revelation
in Mary Lavin's stories most often comes, and her later
work demands even more of the reader's percipience.
'Heart of Gold' is another such story showing narrative
subtlety. The narrative line alternates between scenes
in Lucy's mind, Lucy acting out her ideas with others in
dialogue, and Lucy fabricating scenes from the past and
acting them out in her own mind as a form of interior
dramatic narration. Occasionally a neutral omniscient
passage is inserted as a narrative bridge between the two
dialogue passages separated in time, but for the most
part the author enters deeply into the mind of Lucy
through the latter's interior monologue, which the
reader interprets in relation to what has been revealed
of Lucy through her exterior action. Lucy's self-awareness grows as the story progresses and comes to its crux
in the train bearing her away on her honeymoon.

As Mary Lavin thus enters more subtly into the
thoughts and feelings of her characters through the
multiple viewpoint, the complicated articulation of

their reactions reveals them as spiritual beings faced
with ultimate meaninglessness, as moral beings faced
with social condemnation and as biological beings
faced with the annihilation of death. These three
threads of uncertainty affect feeling, and with it the
concept of reality. They are woven into the fabric of
her stories using the shuttle of time, the colours of
different narrative tones and the pattern of descriptive
language.

Within the dominant tone Mary Lavin may be using
in a particular story, descriptive language has always
played an important part. She may convey feeling by
an occasional motif representing the abstract, such as
the snowdrops Sam and Lucy in 'Heart of Gold' wear
for their winter wedding; the symbolic kernel of the
story may be revealed by its title, as in 'The Lilacs'
or, less obviously, in 'The Cuckoo-Spit'; by the naming
of characters as in 'Love is for Lovers' or 'The Pastor
of Six Mile Bush'; descriptive metaphor may adhere to
concrete image, like the worm impaled on the fork
prong in 'The Lost Child'. For the sight of this image
on the retina of the pregnant Renée reacts at an
intuitive level and connects, for the perceptive reader,
with Renée's previous thoughts about her unborn
child. Feeling is sometimes conveyed by simile, as
Lally's prayer in the train ('The Will') described as
'rapid unformed words, that jostled themselves in her
mind like sheaves of burning sparks'.

This is a language of the blood, or senses, of which
Mary Lavin's later work shows increasing use.[7] The
multiplication of echo within Mary Lavin's stories is
something at which she has become ever more adept.
The reader has to be on the alert as he moves from the
simple comparison of Mr Parr's pursed lips to a
chicken's vent ('The Mock Auction'), to the more complicated image of 'their mouths like swinging censers
spilling song to right and left', ('Tom'). Mary Lavin,

from the first, aims to stimulate awareness, and with it an enlarged concept of reality, in the minds of her readers. As she has matured herself, her desire to do this has not diminished.

A more straightforward descriptive device contributing to feeling comes from the use of place. Mary Lavin writes about subtle changes in feeling and emotion, but the scene in which her figures move often reflects, or initiates, feeling, as well as providing a framework within which the story is set. In 'The Green Grave and the Black Grave' the fishermen's state of mind is influenced by their physical environment; in 'The Great Wave' place triggers off the bishop's daydream. Minds of characters may range far back into the past from the actuality in which they find themselves, calling either upon their own memories, or on folk memory. The free-ranging mental association of the characters are only pinioned by the actuality of the story's starting point — the fishermen have to return to their boat; the bishop to his confirmation duties.

Another example of a story in which scene creates atmosphere is taken from 'In the Middle of the Fields', which begins:

> Like a rock in the sea, she was islanded by fields, the heavy grass washing about the house, and the cattle wading in it as in water. Even their gentle stirrings were a loss when they moved away at evening to the shelter of the woods. A rainy day might strike a wet flash from a hay barn on the far side of the river — not even a habitation!

In 'The Small Bequest' the ethereal nature of Miss Tate's garden carries with it an undercurrent of maliciousness. 'The Haymaking', 'A Gentle Soul', 'An Akoulina of the Irish Midlands', 'One Summer' and 'A Likely Story' are some of the stories containing

evocatively important rural description. Like Vera
Traske in 'Happiness' Mary Lavin loves the natural
clutter of nature, which takes sexual difference for
granted and does not exaggerate its importance. But for
her also human beings are as deeply affected by their
environment as they are by their past, and by their
secret fantasies.

A writer whose principal subject matter is states of
feeling must incorporate all levels of consciousness and
Mary Lavin's mythogenic faculty cannot ignore the subconscious state. She claimed in her *Sunday Press* interview with Brid Mahon that she had 'almost total subconscious recall'; a statement which she would need to
explain herself, for can anyone claim to have this? But
that she said such a thing means the subconscious is
important to her. She writes about reality of outward
representation, based on the happenings in individual
lives. This is surface reality, behind lies an inner reality.
Memory is crystallised from an amalgam of the two
which are mutually dependent. This enduring core of
human experience is not something which can be
categorised. It can only be hinted at through the
patterns language uses to convey meanings: the paradox
being that the conscious act of writing overlays and
limits the conveyance of subconscious expression.

Lawrence Durrell, in his morality play *An Irish
Faustus,* sent his Faustus to the heart of hell. Coming
back Faustus says:

> For the first time I knew I was in reality.
> Most of the time
> We are not, d'you see; life as we know it is
> Conditional state,
> And reality prime — why, it hurts.[8]

The temporal universe is 'simply a great hint', a con-
ditional state. Durrell finds this a very Irish view, hence

the play's title.

Mary Lavin has set herself the difficult task of trying, in James Stephens' phrase, to create 'a matrimony of minds'. She wants to do away with the real/unreal, conscious/subconscious duality which so fascinated Yeats, by showing, as Joyce did, how in human feelings one is essentially interpenetrated by the other.

Already in 'At Sallygap'[9] the author makes Manny and Annie's minds reflect the ebb and flow of progressive and regressive consciousness. Each realistic episode in actuality is followed by withdrawal into reflection based on memory, imaginary daydreams or wish fulfilment, or subconscious mental associations.

Manny, as he starts walking back to Dublin, feels elated, then confused. The following lines show one of the many passages in this story which illustrate the transition of mental states:

> The dark hills and the pale sky and the city pricking out its shape upon the sea with starry lights filled him with strangely mingled feelings of sadness and joy. And when the sky flowered into a thousand stars of forget-me-not blue he was strangled by the need to know what had come over him, and having no other way to stem the tide of desolating joy within him, he started to run the way he used to run on the roads as a young lad. And as he ran he laughed out loud to think that he, Manny Ryan, was running along a country road in the dark, not knowing but he'd run into a hedge or a ditch.
>
> Yesterday, if anyone had come to him and suggested that he'd do such a thing, he would have split his sides laughing. And tomorrow, if he were to try and persuade Annie to take a walk out in the country, she'd look at him as if he was daft.

Annie's feelings are quite different. Her fantasies are

based on frustrated emotions, not frustrated spirit of adventure. She married to break the monotony but finds the gentle, self-effacing Manny boring. While she waits for Manny's return she daydreams. First she hopes his coming may cause an emotional outburst, and she desires this. Then the poorhouse hearse passes the door and a picture of a hideously swollen, drowned corpse passes across her mind. She visualises herself at Manny's wake. Subconsciously she wishes his death. A long narrative passage describing the Dublin streets follows, parallel to the sordid image of Dublin visualised by Manny, but so different from it. Annie's idealised pictures of Dublin show that she, beneath her malevolence, is a romantic.

Manny and Annie hope for different things from life, so their sense of reality differs. In this extraordinarily mature story we see the young Mary Lavin already displaying her mastery of technique. After his return Annie's thoughts are intuitively conveyed to Manny in that non-verbal language of silence which pre-dates words:

> Now, looking up into her eyes, his immature and childish fear fell from him, and instead of it there came into his heart a terrible adult fear; a fear that came from his instincts, from his blood.

Manny thinks of murder and violence. The memory of the Wicklow hills fades. He understands Annie has him imprisoned for ever in her hatred.

The fantasising of both these characters, so necessary to them, is partly subconscious but forms an essential part of their feelings which moulds their conscious attitudes and expressions and affects their mutual view. But their fantasies are hidden, so that though living in close physical intimacy they remain emotionally incomprehensible to each other. Which is their real and which their unreal life? That which appears obvious to the outside observer, or that which forms a continuum in their own minds? How each views him or herself, or how each views the other?

The equivocal nature of reality, and a desire to convey the importance of this, remains Mary Lavin's most abiding concern as a writer. She here enters a dense milky way — the unexplored world of psychophysical aesthetics — so no wonder she considers the short story an intellectual medium. As in the work of James Joyce, the dramatic impact of her explorations rests on using the movements of outward physical happening as a skeleton, or frame, upon or within which the real essence of the psychological drama is hung, or contained in temporal fluidity.

The difficulty in the artistic representation of such an enlarged concept of reality is to balance the physical, or concrete, with the psychological, or abstract aspects. It is easy to get carried away either by the exuberant action of the physical, or by the imaginary dimension of the psychological.

Our vision of reality must always include beliefs accepted on trust — the unseen portion of the iceberg. Man's optic of reality is continually shifting, as it varies from culture to culture, and can never be absolute. It is one role of the artist to represent these shifts as seen from within the society of which he forms part. If Mary Lavin emphasises feeling, and includes the inner realities of life, it is because she is protesting against those who attach exaggerated importance to the outer depiction of, say, violence, sex and calamity, the reporting of which nowadays so often illustrates so-called freedom of expression, or constitutes the whole of the news. Looked at in Mary Lavin's way, reporting only the outward results of the internal drama distorts reality. She wants to promote integrity of feeling; link action to motivation; consider violence through the weakness and fear which initiate it; regard sex through tenderness and altruism, not only by way of aberration and lust. The dreams, fears, joys and sadness in this are all dramatic in their own right.[10]

It is evident that Mary Lavin keeps a distance between her readers and her subject matter, but this distance is far greater in her earlier work. The readers she wrote for in the early 1940s were living in a society whose social structures were still rigid from a modern point of view, but the fabric of society was relatively more secure, and communications less developed. Today's readers live in fluid social structures which they continually question: the fabric of society is highly insecure although many are materially better off, and mass media deploy a battery of visual and aural stimuli.

Any serious writer is bound not only to reflect social changes herself, but also to take into account their effect on her readers. Thus Mary Lavin no longer writes about snobberies of class and social position but she can still hang her hat on intellectual egoism, religious proscription and other forms of human pretension. Except in autobiographical work she has moved from portraying a generation previous to her own and lately, in stories like 'The Lost Child' and 'The Shrine', touched on modern controversies such as the role of religion in society, celibacy, abortion, free love and the female position, but in such an oblique and restrained way that there is always the danger that readers used to being bludgeoned into awareness will either ignore or misinterpret her implications. Her major concerns, however, go beyond social criticism and remain very much the same as they were in early stories such as 'At Sallygap', 'Brother Boniface' and 'The Long Ago'.

She still attempts to relate now with then, memory and past remain an inescapable part of our daily lives which we must face and understand, even if the result is painful. The following passage from 'One Evening', when young Larry comes in to his mother, sitting alone in the dark after the abrupt departure of her husband, shows this woman's pitiful attempt to turn the clock back:

> Not for years had the piano been opened . . . . And, when she began to pull off the heavy, handmade runner that covered the instrument all over like an altar cloth, he shrank into himself at the thought of the queer, light-coloured wood of the casing being exposed with its birdy-eyes graining and its curli-cues. Pianos weren't made of that kind of wood any more.
>
> And so, before a note was struck, he braced him-self for the unpleasant sounds that would come from the damp and stuck-together keys . . . . But things were worse than he'd feared; when his mother ran her hand up and down the notes neither bass nor treble was discernible under the knocking sound of the wooden hammers from which the motheaten felting had worn away. Not noticing that anything was wrong, however, his mother began playing with both hands, without music, throwing her head back, her body swaying in time to the notes.

Mary Lavin has told us that her stories develop from the nucleus of an idea, which is a question, injected into a person or an incident, the whole then englobed in some kind of a plot. This genesis sounds simpler than it is, for it all depends on the nature of the question being asked, and to what extent the character personifying the question may take charge of and alter it during the artistic process. Many of Mary Lavin's questions are recurrent ones, such as the effect of time on human ephemerality, a theme illustrated once again in a recent story 'Eterna', the title of which is allusively connected to the subtle time/reality theme.

The evanescent magic of memory plays a large part in Mary Lavin's work, in all those stories set in the days of her mother's youth, her own youth, or in more recent autobiographical work such as 'Happiness' or 'Tom'. We are each of us what the past has made us, and the frequent use of memory reflects both her personal fascination with it, and the importance she attaches to it. Memory mingles fact and fantasy, filling the gaps and embroidering the edges of actuality. Memory is both fluid and imprecise but it binds. The world of feeling about which Mary Lavin writes can be confined to neither the concrete nor the actual, for reality must comprise far more than the here and now. About this, as she matures, Mary Lavin has become more adamant than ever. In this her ideas coincide with those of 'modernism', defined as not so much technical or perceptual development as a discovery that reality is no more than personal.

5 The Significance of Textual Revisions

In her recent *Irish Times* interview Mary Lavin expressed clear views on the necessity for sometimes editing or re-writing her own work:

> American universities invite writers on campus to teach young people how to write. If you have anything to teach there is another way in which you teach it, by making corrections in your own early work. Providing always that the corrections improve. There is always a possibility that you may spoil a story . . . there is a contradictory theory which I hold myself that if improved too much you reach a kind of perfection which, like beauty in a woman, can be too perfect. You lose impetuosity and liveliness.
>
> On the other hand nobody wants to leave slovenly work behind them. If you get a chance, and if you have the time, I don't see why you shouldn't correct. In my case there is another point, that when I was very young I doubt if I made many drafts at all. I sat down and dashed off a story, and in the early books, for all to see, although people don't seem to

notice it, there are incredible mistakes and flaws . . . .

An analysis of Mary Lavin's alterations to her earlier stories for publication in the London collected edition shows that some have not been altered, or contain only a few minor cuts; another group have been re-styled for paragraphing, punctuation and to tighten up their impact; only a few stories have been virtually re-written.

It will be convenient, for the purposes of analysis, to classify alterations under six categories, which are not mutually exclusive:

(1) changes in detail, names of characters, places and descriptive background.
(2) layout — paragraphing, punctuation and sentence structure,
(3) narrative or authorial comment,
(4) style,
(5) change in emphasis related to the author's own development,
(6) change in emphasis related to artistic intent.

A consideration of some specific stories, the alterations to which may fall under several of these headings, reveals in what way Mary Lavin found weakness in her earlier work and at the same time indicates how her own perspective may have altered with the passing years. Changes under the first four headings are technical rather than artistic, made at the objectively critical level; alterations in emphasis are sometimes more complicated and may show a shift in perspective.

* * *

Three stories which exemplify change in small concrete details are 'The Green Grave and the Black Grave',

'A Wet Day' and 'The Small Bequest'.

In 'The Green Grave and the Black Grave' all the names of characters are altered except that of Tadg Mor. His son Tadg Beag (small Tadg) becomes Tadg Og (young Tadg). There seems no reason for these changes other than one of euphony, as a comparative reading aloud of the following passages shows:

(first version)
'It was seven weeks before Lorcan MacKinealy was got and his eye sockets emptied by the gulls and the gannies.'

(second version)
'It was seven weeks before Maolshaughlin O'Dalaigh was got and his eye sockets emptied by the gulls and the gannies'.

The second name is softer and also more representative of the sound of breaking waves with which the finding of the bodies ashore would be associated. The same reason for changing Sean-Bhean O Suilleabheain to Seana Bhride could be supposed, it reads more musically in the context and this story is full of internal rime.

In 'A Wet Day' Father Gogarty becomes Father Gogan. He wants to preach on hygiene not on avoiding colds; the money raised by the parishioners is to be spent not on silk banners with gilt tassels, brass candelabra and yards of confraternity ribbon with fringes and picot edging, but on sodality banners, altar linen, vestments and new surplices. The vegetables pressed on Fr Gogan in version two are of a much wider variety than in version one. These changes, apart from the priest's name which may have been made for personal reasons, update the story sociologically.

The second version of 'The Small Bequest' moves the locale of the family from Rattigan Rowe to Clyde Road,

Ballsbridge, in Dublin. All such small alterations may be
made for euphony, and/or to create realistic social
background. There are many other examples, such as
the removal of SAG (St Anthony Guide) — an invoca-
tion which used to be put on the back flaps of
envelopes) — from the second version of 'The Nun's
Mother', removed no doubt because it is obscure to non-
catholic readers and is no longer used except by school-
girls.

* * *

Under the heading of layout Mary Lavin has made
frequent alterations to paragraphing in her earlier work,
but mainly in the heavily re-written stories.

'The Long Holidays', from the later volume *The
Patriot Son* in which the stories have generally been re-
edited very little for subsequent publication, has been
substantially altered to increase the narrative tempo.
The narrative tone has also been altered by the addition
of 'would':

1956 text
'How do you ever get things to fit you!' they cried.
'Fancy having to have everything altered!'

And the married ones were the worst. One day one
of them leant over her and whispered into her ear.
'I suppose it's *deliberately* you never got married?'

And the implications were so enormous and undiscoverable to her, that she was frightened to death
for weeks. Because, of course, it was not deliberately
at all.

1974 text
'How do you ever get things to fit you?' they'd cry.
'Fancy having to have everything made or altered!'

The married ones were the worse. 'I suppose it's
deliberately you never got married?' one of them

whispered into her ear one day. The implications of this seemed so enormous, yet at the same time so undiscoverable to Dolly, that she was frightened to death for weeks. Because, of course, it was not deliberate at all.

It is evident from the ending of another edited early story, 'Sarah', that Mary Lavin has improved her ability to control the telling pause in dialogue:

1943 text
Oliver said nothing, but his limbs stiffened with resentment. His wife watched him closely and she clenched her hands.

'You can spare your sympathy. She won't need it'. Oliver looked up.

'Did she stay out all night in the rain?'

'She did', said Kathleen, and she stared at him. 'At least that's where they found her in the morning, as dead as a rat, and the child dead beside her!'

Her pale eyes held him. His own eyes stared uncomprehendingly into them. She began to move back into the house away from his stare. He looked down at her hand that held the tin of red sheep-raddle.

'Give me the raddle!' he said, and before she had time to hand it to him he repeated it, again and again, frantically.

'Give me the raddle. Give it to me. Hurry, will you! Give me the Godamn' stuff'.

1974 text
Oliver said nothing. His wife watched him closely and she clenched her hands. 'You can spare your sympathy. She won't need it'.

Oliver looked up.

'Where did she go?'

'Nowhere', Kathleen said slowly.

Oliver tried to think clearly. It had been a bad night, wet and windy. 'She wasn't out all night in the rain?' he asked, a fierce light coming into his eyes. 'She was', Kathleen said, and she stared at him. 'At least that's where they found her in the morning, dead as a rat. And the child dead beside her!' Her pale eyes held his, and he stared uncomprehendingly into them. Then he looked down at her hand that held the tin of red sheep-raddle.

'Give me the raddle!' he said, but before she had time to hand it to him he yelled at her again. 'Give me the raddle. Give it to me. What are you waiting for? Give me the God-damn' stuff'.

All such re-writing and editing shows progression in Mary Lavin's craftsmanship and artistic exactitude. Yet it seems she fears too much editorial work will weaken creativity based on instinctive response. For the same reason she fears in her everyday life that practicalities of farm and family may stifle the fragile imaginative growth of her creative endeavour. She is forever in tension between what Virginia Woolf called 'that queer amalgamation of dream and reality, that perpetual marriage of granite and rainbow'. The same tension exists when it comes to editing her own work which, written years before, is almost like editing the work of another.

* * *

Direct authorial intervention, or the intrusive presence of the author, is a common fault among young writers. With Mary Lavin it takes more often the form of inconsistent narrative tone, when the author/narrator tone invades that of the character/narrator. Removal of such intrusion and a supervision of the probability and consistence of narrative tone were evidently two faults Mary Lavin recognised to be present in some of her early work. The story 'Lemonade', not so far re-published, would need substantial alteration on these grounds.

Three stories, otherwise unchanged, from which con-clusive narrative remarks have been removed in the reprinted versions are 'A Single Lady', 'Posy' and 'Chamois Gloves'.

'A Single Lady' originally had tacked on at the end of the sentence: 'Among the many attributes of the intellect the power to fathom that glance was not numbered. Its import was for ever hidden from her; an educated, intellectual, and highly developed single lady.' The author/narrator here laid heavy stress on the ironic content of the story, already quite sufficiently evident to the reader.

'Posy' had its original final phrase, 'And now he need no longer guess! He knew', removed for the same reason. The author/narrator tone intruded to emphasise the obvious.

The reprinted 'Chamois Gloves' drops the final whim-sical paragraph and ends with Veronica going to sleep. This has the effect of laying less stress on the element of fantasy in the religious aspect of the story than the original ending, which was: 'But over her head, high above the roof and cupola, loud, loud, loud, could she but hear it, the bells of heaven were ringing out her sacrifice.' Mary Lavin seems very aware of avoiding didacticism.

She wrote a few early fables, 'The Sand Castle', 'A Fable', 'The Rabbit' and 'The Bunch of Grape', in which waves, a briar, a rabbit and grapes are used as central images, or what she calls 'devices of concentration', round which the allegorical element takes shape. Other-wise her theme is generally well embedded in irony or objective compassion, to the extent that the interpreta-tion of it is often left to the reader's choice. As in life, we must come to our own conclusions.

* * *

The re-writing of some stories, apart from layout, has been undertaken for the purpose of clarifying style and impact. 'Brother Boniface', 'Sunday brings Sunday' and 'The Long Ago' all exemplify this.

Two short comparative passages from 'Brother Boniface' illustrate Mary Lavin's careful re-writing of parts of this story:

1943 text
And Barney was frightened because he couldn't remember looking at anything but the big red-chalked barrels, and the dry dusty boards, and the great steaming nostrils of the cattle. He had been looking at them all the time, and if he looked away it could only have been for a minute when a wisp of scarlet cloud floated out between the chimney of the barrack and the spire of the church. The cloud had only floated there for a moment, before it was blown out of sight, but it was such a strange and beautiful colour that Barney had stared at it. And when he cried with his head in his mother's lap it was not because he was beaten, but because he began to feel faintly that there was something odd about himself, and that ordinary successful people, people who were respected in this town, like his own father, would never be foolish enough to stand with their hands down by them, doing nothing, as he longed to do, for hours and hours, just staring at the trees or the grasses or the stars or the rains.

1974 text
And he was frightened because he couldn't remember looking at anything else but the big red-chalked barrels, and the dusty boards, and the great steam-

ing nostrils of the cattle. He was looking at them all the time, and if he looked away it could only have been for a second when in the grey dawn a wisp of scarlet cloud floated out between the chimney of the barrack and the spire of the church. But later in the morning when he was thinking things over it seemed to him that there might be something odd about him, and that ordinary successful people — people who were respected in the town, like his own father — would never be foolish enough to stand and stare at a cloud.

The second version is more pragmatic and concise, which heightens the irony, but this story as a whole has lost something in the re-writing, as another short paragraph illustrates more clearly:

1943 text
Life went flashing by the monastery, leaves and petals were blown past the uncurtained windows, trees tossed in the wind, and webs of rain were spun across the glass. The skies shook out their gay confetti of stars. Brother Boniface stepped into his sandals some twenty thousand mornings, and the days slipped by so fast that one fine morning he was eighty years old.

1974 text
Time went flashing past fast as the wind, and life was blown with it as the wind blew the leaves from the trees. And Brother Boniface had stepped into his sandals some twenty thousand mornings before he realised one fine morning that he was eighty years old.

The first passage has a joyous insouciance and leisure which the second lacks, and conveys better the rapid passing of Brother Boniface's uneventful days in peaceful surroundings, fleeting shadows of time amid the aeons of the universe. A close comparative analysis of the two versions of this subtle story — much too lengthy to undertake here — would make a profitable exercise for the tyro short story writer.

In 'Sunday brings Sunday' there is evidence throughout of the style being speeded up. For instance the phrase, 'everyone acted with the deliberation of actors' becomes the brisk, 'the people moved like actors in a play'. There is the same tendency as in 'Brother Boniface' to pare down poetic content, creating a more concise text.

The editing of this story has also clarified its impact. Mad Mary, old hag of the second version, no longer rubs the lichen off the writings on old tombstones. Previously described as uttering a chant of 'weariness and sorrow', this becomes in the second version 'wariness and sorrow', a significant change which has the effect of making her less of a lunatic, and more of a prophetic figure. In the second text the narrator stands back. Compare sentences such as: 'Mona always had the best altar in the village' (1943), with 'Didn't she herself always have the best altar in the village' (1974). Mary Lavin has also paid attention to the adjectives describing the priest. The first version has 'the light glittering evilly' and 'the vicious light glittering' on the priest's glasses; in the second version 'evilly' and 'vicious' are both removed. 'The cold sermon with long Latin words' (1943) becomes 'the long sermon with familiar Latin words' (1974). The removal of these pejorative adjectives makes the priest neutral. He is now as much a victim of ignorance as the people. These changes are related both to style and also to the author clarifying her intent by a subtle alteration in dramatic emphasis.

'The Long Ago' has been heavily re-edited. An erroneous 'Aggie' who crept into the first version is removed. The confidential 'you see' is dropped from the following passage. The revised version is less rambling, more matter-of-fact:

1944 text
It had been a difficult situation for Blossom too, but as events turned out the situation settled itself; for in a short time Blossom encountered another difficulty and one drove out the other as fire drives out fire. You see, Blossom got married again, and her second husband, unlike Dominie, was a big assertive fellow that would not let her out of his sight, but made her go everywhere with him; hanging on his arm. It was awkward to visit the grave of a first husband on the arm of a second, particularly when the gates were so narrow that two people could not possibly pass through without unlinking. So Blossom gave up going there at all. She had a first-class headstone erected over the grave and left it at that. The grave was all Hallie's then.

1974 text
The situation could have been difficult for Blossom too if matters had not settled themselves unexpectedly. Because a short time after Dominie's death Blossom married again. And unlike Dominie, her second husband was a big, assertive fellow who would not let Blossom out of his sight. She was always hanging from his arm. And since the main gates of the cemetery were kept locked except on the days of funerals, and the side gates were so narrow two people could not go through linked, Blossom soon gave up visiting the grave. She ordered a headstone to be erected, and never went near the cemetery again. The grave was all Hallie's after that.

The narrative tone of this story has been altered, as is

perhaps more evident from the following passage:

1944 text
Just as the leafy boughs of springtime and youth
were about to enclose her with their fragrance in the
small malodorous parlour of Ella's house, Hallie was
recalled to where she was by a piercing scream that
sounded far off in a room on the upper floor.

1974 text
For a moment as Hallie sat there in the stuffy parlour
it seemed to her that the leafy boughs of youth and
springtime were about to form a bower about her,
when, abruptly she was recalled to her whereabouts
by a piercing scream. Oliver was gone!

In the first version events are narrated in a dreamlike
fashion, as if they have already occurred. In the second
version the scene is presented more graphically. The
second narrative tone shows greater neutrality on the
part of the omniscient narrator whose stance is, however, right in front of Hallie, no longer regarding her
distantly down the tunnel of time.

The first version of this story does tend to ramble
but in making it more actualized and concise it seems
Mary Lavin has cut out too much of the evanescent
atmosphere based on the ebb and flow of dream and
reality. In the first version when at the end of the story
Hallie makes the tactless remark to the just-widowed
Ella, Ella pushes her violently backwards and we see the
result through Hallie's dreamlike illusion of time:

And then all around her it seemed that people were
talking all in the same tone, and all saying the same
thing.
   'Hush, Ella. Hush. She didn't mean it. She didn't
know what she was saying'.

And the past that had flashed so green around her, vanished as suddenly as it had come. She was standing in Ella's parlour under the lamp in the middle of the room. And Ella was screaming worse than before and struggling against the people who tried to make her sit down on the sofa.

In the second version the practical tone cuts out the illusion within Hallie's mind. Ella no longer pushes her and we see only her close-up, exterior:

But almost before she finished, Ella broke away from her, and began to scream again and to struggle to get out of the room again. Her mother had to take hold of her and try to pacify her.

'Don't mind her, Ella. She didn't mean it', she said. 'She didn't know what she was saying'.

What was the matter? What had she said? Hallie looked around for Dolly. But Dolly was staring at her with eyes that would take the heat out of the sun.

The first version of the story lays more stress on Hallie, romantic dreamer; the second version on Hallie the spinster. The title of the story is more in keeping with its original text.

Such changes lead to the conclusion that Mary Lavin the elder has with her greater technical mastery, lost a little of her strength to dream.

* * *

Changes in emphasis related to the author's own development and changes in emphasis related to artistic intent cannot be distinguished with any exactitude, unless an obviously autobiographical element ' is involved. This occurs in the story, 'Say could that lad be I?'

The first version of this story (published 1941) was
written before Mary Lavin's father died. When revising
the story for its 1974 publication she re-wrote the intro-
ductory preamble describing her father, who then takes
over as first person narrator of an incident from his own
youth. The second version still opens; 'This is my
father's story. It isn't mine at all.' Then the two versions
differ:

1941 text
When I am in Dublin I think of him as I have so
often seen him, standing in a dusty yellow field, or a
green field tufty with clover clumps, staring at a
cropping beast, or just walking along scotching thistle
with a walking stick.

My father is always busy with his hands, tying back
a rambling briar that would scratch the eyes out of
the galloping colts, or pulling down the choking strings
of ivy from the bark of a young tree. In Meath a
man must restrain the lovely fertile land, or it will
strangle him with its greenery. But in Roscommon,
where my father was born, the fields capriciously
point up their chaste rocks through the grass and
defy man to win them wholly to his way.

1974 text
When I think of him, I think of him as I so often saw
him, walking green fields dusty with buttercups,
stopping only to stare at his prize cattle, cropping
the rich grass, or to scotch a thistle with a blade he
had fitted to the butt of his walking-stick. His eye
was always quick to see the weeds that seemed to
spring up overnight, and which, if left uncut, self-
sowed themselves and multiplied seven times seven.
In Meath a man must restrain the land, or it would
strangle him. But in Roscommon, where he was
born, the fields were thin and the grass wiry and

sparse.

It is interesting to compare these texts and see how Mary Lavin's memory of her father now paints the scene differently. Thistle and weeds take the place of briar and ivy; but who, least of all the author herself, could say what subconscious process caused the different images to arise?

An intrusive authorial comment occurs in the first version:

> Perhaps we are different people, all of us, from the children we once were, as we are different people from the men we dream ourselves to be. Perhaps when we sit and think of things we did long ago there is no idle egoism in our musings, but rather the unselfishness of thoughts about another person; a person we once knew.

This is removed from the second version. Here, as a young writer, Mary Lavin reveals an interest in what was to become one of her pervading themes. The effect of time on memory — the fascination with the rich soil of the past in which the present is rooted in a mysterious way difficult to define; the difference between the actual and the idealised self.

The rest of this story shows only small changes in style and punctuation caused by attention to narrative tone, rendering it more consistent with the outlook of a young boy narrator.

From the re-telling of this story we can see what Arthur Koestler has called the trinity of the artistic process, selection, exaggeration and simplification. He explains that:

> Even the most naturalistic picture, chronicle, or novel, whose maker naively hopes to copy reality,

contains an unavoidable element of bias, of selective emphasis. Its direction depends on the distorting lenses in the artist's mind — the perceptual and conceptual matrices which pattern his experience, and determine which aspects of it should be regarded as relevant, which not. This part-automatic, part-conscious processing of experience, over which the medium exercises a kind of 'feedback-control', determines to a large extent what we call an artist's individual style.[1]

It is obvious that any author re-editing his own work twenty or more years after it was first written will no longer be looking at life through an identical distorting lens. Events, experience and his own maturity are all factors tending to alter his selective emphasis. Writing new material is quite a different process from revising what has already been written long before. When first writing he selects facts from memory, using whatever exaggeration or simplification his experience and imagination tell him will be most effective; when re-writing the facts are pre-selected. They were, he knows, a *mèlange* based on memory and imagination, but only he knows in what proportion. He now absorbs his work as the reader does and the changes of emphasis he makes to it alter the original decisions on exaggeration or simplification according to his present perceptual judgment. It is perhaps because the tension between old style and new are so often insurmountable that most writers avoid re-writing after a long period. Even within a short time difference they prefer, as Joyce did with *Stephen Hero* and the *Portrait*, to create kindred but dissimilar works.[2]

Major textual changes hinge on alterations in emphasis based on a more mature artistic judgment, either because Mary Lavin finds the original text lacks clarity of impact; or because her own idea of what should be exaggerated or simplified has altered with passing time. As has already been shown from the passages taken from 'Brother Boniface' and 'The Long Ago', the desire to increase clarity sometimes removes an evanescent atmosphere present in the first version. But the stories 'An Akoulina of the Irish Midlands' and 'At Sallygap' illustrate the interaction of changes in emphasis which result in an improved text.

In 'An Akoulina of the Irish Midlands' there are a number of small clarifying text changes such as the specific mention of 'The Tryst' as the Turgenev story to which the title refers, and there are three changes in emphasis: (1) the first person narrator, originally female, becomes male; (2) Andy Hackett, the 'misogynist' becomes a 'misogamist'; (3) in version one Lena's inner voice is the 'oracle within her, whose word to her was law' while in version two this is altered to 'suddenly it was as if there was a Third Person there with us in the little pantry – one who spoke more wisely than I and to whom Lena was listening'. The use of 'suddenly' and the capital letters implies the Holy Spirit, whose sevenfold gifts include wisdom and understanding. This nuance elevates Lena's ability to love onto a higher plane than one prescribed by, and vaguely emanating from, an 'oracle'.

Giving this story a male narrator, a paternal figure in whom Lena confides, instead of the same role being played by a presumably middle-aged female, alters the emphasis to one of greater sympathy with Lena. Most readers will subconsciously presume an elderly male narrator to be more experienced in the male implications of the Andy/Lena relationship. Andy's lustful intentions are thus less equivocally implied. That Andy is now called a misogamist, a hater of marriage rather than of women, explicitly suggests his dishonourable intentions. Mary Lavin must have made such deliberate changes in emphasis because she thought the first version of the story ambiguous.

When we come to 'At Sallygap', which remains one of the best Lavin stories, the author's alterations to the first text are multiple and include changes made under all six headings of the analytical categories being considered. A few specific comparisons will illustrate this.

The two different openings show the less leisurely narrative tempo of the second version; some adjectives have been removed and the punctuation and phraseology changed. In the second paragraph the hovering author/narrator withdraws and the feminine ending of 'defiantly' is cut to the more erect 'defiant' followed by the alliterative 'pale pasture'. Such passages typify the careful attention Mary Lavin often pays to artistic, apart from factual, impact.

1943 text

The red-and-white bus climbed up the hilly roads on its way, through the Dublin Mountains, to the town of Enniskerry. On either side the hedges were so high and heavy that the passengers had nothing more interesting to look at than each other, but after a short time the road became steeper than before. Then the fields that had been hidden by hedges were all bared to view, and slanted smoothly downward to the edge of the distant city. Dublin was all exposed. The passengers told each other that you could see every inch of it. They would certainly see every steeple and every tower. But, had they admitted as much, they would have said that the dark spires and steeples that rose up out of the blue pools of distance below looked little better than dark thistles rising up defiantly in a gentle pasture.

1974 text

The bus climbed up the hilly roads on its way through the Dublin Mountains to the town of Enniskerry.

On either side the hedges were so high that the passengers had nothing more interesting to look at than each other. But after a short time the road became steeper and then the fields that had been hidden were bared to view, slanting smoothly downward to the edge of the distant city. Dublin was all exposed. The passengers could see every inch of it. They could certainly see every steeple and tower, although as these spires and steeples rose up out of the blue pools of distance they looked little more than dark thistles rising up defiant in a pale pasture.

An altered Manny is introduced into the second version when he appears as seen through the eyes of the stranger on the bus. This Manny has an expression of 'depth' (not dignity) in his eyes; 'cockiness' (not 'urgent respectability') is the air given by his striped city suiting, and his bowler hat is no longer 'very slightly mildewed'. The result is that instead of the shabbily dignified Charlie Chaplinesque figure of the first version Manny now exudes pathos, with a tinge of bravura.

The whole of Manny's interior monologue, except for those passages he speaks aloud, has in the second version been couched in the third person. This creates a more consistent point of view and removes the uncertain note of mockery present in the exclamatory phrase:

He looked at the gleaming grass in the wet ditch, and at the flowers and flowering reeds that grew there. 'They all have names I suppose', thought Manny. Could you beat that!

In the second version, without quotes, 'he thought' replaces 'thought Manny', and the final exclamatory phrase is thus brought within Manny's narrative tone.

Perhaps from tact Mary Lavin has in her second

version removed Manny's opinion that, 'All Dublin people were good for was talking, they'd talk you out of your mind!' Her own experience as a non-quiescent mother may have caused her to query the appropriateness of: 'Annie Ryan's nature was too fierce for the quiescent passions of love and motherhood', which is dropped from the 1974 text.

Annie's interior monologue has been carefully amended and all phrases which, though attractive, were improbably contained within it, removed. For example:

> The city evening was so fair and so serene, so green and blue and gilt, that she disliked looking at it, for it threatened to rob her of all her dreads and deluge her fears with the sane waters of hope.

becomes simply:

> The evening was so fair and so serene, so green and gilt, it threatened to rob her of all her dreads and soothe her fears.

The alliterative outburst, too sensitive to come from Annie's mind:

> She saw herself at the wake, moaning and rocking from side to side at the fire, fanged with the yellow teeth of remorse and mauled by memories.

becomes:

> She saw herself at the wake, moaning and rocking from side to side, with everyone pitying her.

The overall effect of the carefully edited second version is to create a tighter, rather brisk, narrative structure; a more consistent narrative tone; the author withdraws and the change of emphasis makes Manny a more tragic and less ridiculous figure. The second version reflects both the greater technical mastery and the more mature compassion of an older Mary Lavin.

The changes of emphasis made to the three early stories Mary Lavin has most radically re-written — 'The Young Girls' (1944), 'The Nun's Mother' (1944) and 'A Woman Friend' (1951) — tend to confirm the ironic and metaphoric implications so far unravelled in this study. More compassion is shown for the simple adolescent characters in 'The Young Girls' than for the mature and well-educated Dr Lew of 'A Woman Friend' or Mrs Latimer of 'The Nun's Mother'. Mary Lavin evidently believes that the greater the level of awareness — whether innate, or achieved from opportunity for self-improvement — the greater the responsibility towards members of the intimate circle as well as to society at large. Expedient morals and the essential selfishness of human motive remain, nevertheless, rebarbative aspects of behaviour. Education, experience and comfortable living standards seem to hinder rather than help her characters to expand their self-awareness. The way she has re-written these three stories makes this clear.

In the 1964 version of 'The Young Girls' Emily and her young friends appear more obviously childish. The following description of the girls' impressions as they look out of the open window show them in the 1964 version to be merely shy, no longer even thinking about the future:

1944 text
And as they stood there a sadness fell on them, inexplicably, and with it a great reluctance to go downstairs at all. In their hearts they wished that this moment would last for ever. As they stood there, at the open window, it seemed that youth was a brightly lighted place, like the room in which they stood;

fragrant, simple and pleasant, but that life was dark
as the dark world outside, wilful as the strong river,
and as fierce, relentless and unknowable as the night
fowl that screamed in his secretive place down among
the reeds.

1964 text
And as they stood there shyness stole over them
again, and they felt a great reluctance to go downstairs at all. If only they could stay up here — for
ever.

When the girls later got up from contemplating their
chastity on the cold rim of the porcelain bath they are,
in the first version, still in the dreamy realms of
romance, so that to them 'the strands of music began
to unwind in the air and seemed to twine in and out
through the banister rails', reminiscent of the serpent in
the tree of knowledge. In the 1964 text this has been
replaced by:

The bathroom door was always a bit swollen from
steam and they had to tug at it to get it open, but
when it opened the music rushed up like a geyser,
rushed and gushed, and now and then the pianist
ran a hand over the treble and little jets flowed up-
ward and played in the air like a fountain.

In the second version the tightened dramatic move-
ment of the dialogue, between Emily's brother Harry
and Ursula, illustrates the more pragmatic, slightly
jocular tone pervading the re-written text:

1944 text
'Come on!' said Harry, 'let us hurry'. Nell was
nowhere to be seen. Ursula was going out the hall
door with Harry, when they caught sight of Emily,

who had been cut off from them in the hall. 'Quick, before Emily sees us', said Harry, and Ursula's heart beat faster still. 'Where are you going, Ursula? Ursula! Harry!' Emily had seen them after all, but just as she was going to run after them, her mother stopped her.

1964 text
'Oh great!' cried Harry. 'Let's hurry'. Nell was nowhere to be seen. As they went out the hall door they caught sight of Emily.

'Quick, before she sees us!' said Harry. Too late.

'Where are you going, you two?' cried Emily. 'Ursula! Harry! Wait for me'. And she started to run after them when her mother rose like a pillar of cloud, right in her way.

The second version of the story, though technically superior to the first version, contains less effective evocativeness. The unstable, romantic and uninformed nature of the adolescent girls' minds is stressed, but the mysterious and impending doom of their budding womanhood recedes into the background, and this dimension of the story is lost. Is this due to the difference between Mary Lavin childless, and Mary Lavin mother of three young daughters? Or is it also because the stress on the female burden and inescapable destiny have lessened during these twenty years? The fickle behaviour they show towards each other and the boys at the party now appears a part of their childishness, rather than a part of their subordinate status as females. It is clearly impossible here to separate changes in emphasis which stem from the author's own development and from her conscious artistic intent.

The rewritten text of 'A Woman Friend', about one thousand words longer than the earlier version, contains altered professional facts about Dr Lew, more circumstantial detail on events leading up to the patient's death, and greater ironical emphasis of the doctor's egoism, for instance:

> If he hadn't been under such a strain already, he wouldn't have paid any heed to the poor wretched woman. (mother of the dead boy)

becomes:

> If he hadn't been under such strain already he would hardly have been so apprehensive of an enquiry or so worried about its findings. Not with his reputation!

In the second version Dr Lew returns to the hospital for a last look at the boy after visiting Bina, and then tells the hospital he will be available at any time during the night. This makes it clear he considered the boy to be extremely ill, and his guilt at falling asleep in the car outside his house is consequently greater. The second version also develops in much greater detail, with additional anecdotes, Dr Lew's habit of napping, or pretending to nap, in odd places, and his own smugness at his operating brilliance.

In the first version there is an inconsistent reaction, removed in the second, when it says (of Dr Lew), 'for a moment he had an almost overpowering longing to bury his face in Bina's bosom', related two pages later to (of Bina), 'the longing came in her again to press his head into the soft moist flannelette bosom'. In version two Dr Lew admits that in addition to Bina being his good friend, she is the only friend he has.

The change of emphasis in this story is not one of direction but of additional weight; by the selection of more detail delineating Dr Lew and by clearer exaggeration of events leading up to the emotional crux round which the story is written. Of this character — more appropriately than of Manny in 'At Sallygap' — it could be said, 'he disgusts himself'. The whole effect is to make Lew Anderson more responsible and so more culpable, self-centred and smug than he at first appeared. The ironic implications of the story are correspondingly accentuated.

In 'The Nun's Mother' the extensive re-writing results in a much longer story, and conveys many subtle changes in emphasis. The two versions produce two different Mrs Latimers, the changes in whom are related not only to the changes of emphasis Mary Lavin consciously wishes to convey but also, in Koestler's words, to 'the perceptual and conceptual matrices which pattern' her artist's distorting lens, when she comes to re-edit the story some thirty years after it was first written.

There is first a change in the 'anatomy of composition'. The revised version introduces more rhetorical emphasis by breaking up paragraphing, clarifying punctuation and changing phrases. The flat statement: 'A nun to pray for her. That meant the prayers of her daughter Angela', becomes: 'A Nun to pray for her? Her daughter Angela! Such a notion! It was utterly absurd'.

'Prayers of remorse' become 'prayers of contrition', a weaker word. The emphatic dashes introduced into this early paragraph and the large number of exclamation marks in the re-edited text have the effect of slowing down the reading speed and stressing the ironic content.

In both versions, Mrs Latimer is credited with similar feelings about women's 'strange triumph' when they hear of a call to the celibate life because of their 'curious streak of chastity', but the first Mrs Latimer emerges as vague, inconsequential but imaginative and emotional. She thinks of the housewife:

They flicked the dish-cloths from them, from time to

time, sending fans of filigree spray into the warm
kitchen air, and all the time their minds were filled
with conquering visions of glad young girls (who
might have been themselves) going garlanded with
lilies down a cool green cloistered arch ivied over by
the centuries; and, what was more, those glad young
girls were going without once looking back at the
blazing lawns, lit with brightly burning sun and
hotly flaming flowers where lovers with lutes were
lying.

The second, disillusioned, impatient, Mrs Latimer of the
same passage is less alliterative, more prosaic:

For no reason at all they'd flick a dishcloth irritably
in the air and send a mist of fine rain through the hot
kitchen, their minds invaded by visions of green girls
(who might have been themselves) going garlanded
with lilies (or white flowers of some kind) down
cloisters ivied over by centuries. And these young
girls would be going away gladly, without once
looking backward to where, behind them on summer
lawns, and sunny river banks, others, with lovers,
lay dallying.

The first Mrs Latimer, possessed of a more lively
imagination than the second, is shown to be more
sensitive to the feelings of others, especially those of her
husband Luke. The second Mrs Latimer, whose self-
centredness emerges in the long opening passage, makes
her husband appear slightly ridiculous. In the first
version she hesitates to shock Luke by showing him her
eyes, 'empty of hurt, empty of sorrow'. In the second
version she is afraid to show Luke that her eyes are
'empty — empty, that was to say, of all appropriate
expression', but she does not reveal what that expression might be.

That Luke is differently portrayed by the two Mrs Latimers emerges from the following comparative passages:

1944 text
There now. That was the truth. That was what she really felt about it. Not grief or sorrow in her loss, and not pride and joy either in the fact that the Lord had chosen the fruit of her tree. To be quite honest, she didn't believe He had *chosen* Angela. Angela had *gone.* But why? There was the mystery. Angela had made her choice and gone away without thinking of them, without caring how they felt it seemed. And now there was Luke with tears in his eyes. And there was she herself — a nun's mother.

1974 text
There now! That was the truth. That was what she felt about the whole business — disbelief. Not grief. And certainly not the joy which was what some people seemed to think she ought to feel! As for pride that the Lord should have chosen the fruit of her womb! Well, to be perfectly honest she did not believe He had chosen Angela. Angela had taken it into her head and gone. But why? Why? That was what Mrs. Latimer hadn't been able to discover. The girl had made her choice alone, without once consulting them, and calmly announced her decision without caring — it would seem — how badly they felt. And here was poor Luke — Mrs. Latimer did not need to glance at him, she knew how he'd look — here he was sitting beside her in the cab, like a dummy.

The reasons behind her feelings are carefully gone into. The first Mrs Latimer appears less dogmatic and more sympathetic than the second.

'Are you sure she knows her own mind', Luke asks
each night for six nights upon entering their bedroom.
This association of the question with the site of their
sex life is in the re-edited text altered to his asking the
question in unspecified places 'a hundred times'. The
first Mrs Latimer feels impatience that Luke 'could not
take up where she had failed to find out why their
lovely Angela was going away from them for ever and
ever'. The second Mrs Latimer blames Luke: 'Why
hadn't he seen she had mismanaged her end of the
thing? Why hadn't he taken up where she had failed?
Why hadn't he himself gone to Angela and (with a
masterfulness he had shown himself to be capable
enough of when she was a child) asked her out right
what they both wanted so desperately to know, why she
— their lovely, lovely Angela — was going away and
leaving them for ever? and ever!'

In version one Mrs Latimer asks herself, 'Should she
have spoken to her, straight out, about her body and the
bodies of men?' In version two Mrs Latimer does not
ask herself this direct question because she is too tired
to care: 'Angela had become a regular slave-driver,
whipping her on, and running her off her feet with
preparations for the Big Day'. She does not know
whether Angela knows about sex and her heart 'froze
at the thought of re-opening the whole painful business'.

The second version is also more explicit about sex
and the human body. In version one Mary Lavin was not
herself a mother and the account is presumably based
on her relationship with her own mother: 'a terrible
reticence about the body between mothers and
daughters, a reticence based on revulsion, and not, as
with mothers and sons upon respect and mystery'.
The re-written text corrects this: 'She had always been
conscious of a curious embarrassment — it would not
be going too far to call it revulsion — between herself
and Angela. Well no — not always, but certainly since

the girl reached adolescence'. In the first version Mrs Latimer's doubts about Angela's vocation are based on her fear that Angela does not understand the joys of the flesh she is renouncing. In the second version she tells herself that Angela knows far more than she lets on, and even if they had 'got down to brass tacks' and confronted their daughter together, for 'to do it alone was too much to expect of one parent', she believes Angela would still have entered 'that awful convent'.

A comparison of the two texts of Mrs Latimer's passages of interior monologue about her own sex life with Luke shows the first to be a softer, simpler, more sensitive woman who pays more attention to the religious significance of the religious vocation, and does not flinch from thinking about it. The later Mrs Latimer is harder, more salacious and expedient, dishonest in her thinking, even as she is in life. As the story progresses the second version of the character becomes more clearly the portrayal of a shallow and self-centred middle-aged woman who does not understand the nature of love, and is not fond of anyone but herself.

The first Mrs Latimer, pondering on how she might have explained the nature of true love to her daughter, thinks: 'There were no words to describe it. Those who had tried were exiled and their books burned on the quayside'. This refers perhaps to Irish censorship and the long list of proscribed books. The second version omits this, restricts love to the physical, and is sarcastic about the 'Divine Call'.

The revised version of this story makes Mrs Latimer into a more explicit and less pleasant character, and channels the theme of the story unequivocally into that of a girl entering the religious life in ignorance. In the original text Angela's reasons remain ambiguous, the possibility of a true vocation being one of them, and the mother's idea of love goes far beyond that of sex. Mary Lavin has changed this story from one narrated by an

honest thinking but simple woman, happily married,
who loves and doubts, to one narrated by a self-centred,
spoilt materialist whose husband appears as a silent
'dummy' in the carriage beside her, or in the ridiculous
postures of sex. This change implies a greater stringency
in the criticism of Mrs Latimer's failure in maternal
responsibility. When she revised this story, herself now
a mother, this aspect must have seemed more important,
so Mary Lavin altered the well-meaning but simple to
the deliberately selfish and irresponsible woman who
misquotes 'There had fallen a splendid tear from the
passion tree at the gate'[3] does not understand its
meaning and neglects her female duties.

* * *

The revisions considered in this chapter make it clear
that Mary Lavin feels impelled to re-edit her early work
when it either lacks factual accuracy, stylistic cohesion,
or does not sufficiently convey her aesthetic, and sometimes moral, intention. The original ironic implications
of her work are in general strengthened by these
changes, and the conveyance of feeling is clarified when
changes create a more consistent narrative tone. In some
of her re-editing there is a tendency to diminish or
pare down the original lyrical exuberance, and though
usually the story is improved as a result, sometimes a
poetic allusiveness is lost when the moralist overcomes
the idealist.[4]

Mary Lavin dislikes the process of revising texts,
though as a conscientious artist she feels obliged to do
so. Levels of creativity in writers vary and Mary Lavin's
creative vision is based firmly in the subconscious and
intuitive. This means that memories, feelings, implied
states and unspoken reactions are all subjects for con-
templation. She is also aware that this fragile artistic
urge is subject to continual invasion from everyday
practicalities and vitiated by too much logical analysis.

Conclusion

'If we open a river bed by writing or acting, reality may flow into that river
bed, into a course it would not have taken had we not intervened'.

Nikos Kazantzakis, *Report to Greco*

This study has been concerned more with the referential
than with the linguistic dimension of Mary Lavin's
work. It should now be possible to answer the questions
posed at the start. On the evidence considered, what is
Mary Lavin in mutiny against? And what specific contribution to literature has she made as a short story writer?

The word 'mutiny' conveys active resistance, even
revolt. Mary Lavin has not chosen the more usual path
of the artist who expresses revolt in overt forms of
anger, disgust and violence. She deliberately mutes her
rebellion, though she knows some readers will find this
insipid fare. None of her stories will ever have paper-
covers that sell, showing nudity, decadence, bloodshed
or violence. In modern terminology, she keeps a low
profile.

Writing, as she does, largely about feelings, we have
seen that she condemns the self-centred, materialistic
and insensitive. She is most concerned with two of the
eight deadly sins Konrad Lorenz has attributed to
civilised man, the break with tradition and entropy of
feeling.[1] The break in tradition is that 'generation gap',
an extension of which is the failure to develop historical

imagination, about which so much has been written. It is evident from her work that Mary Lavin is fascinated by fresh perspectives ever forming in the minds of each successive generation; the way in which experience repeats itself, but always within the context of personal reference. The past, and especially family links in the past, are for her essential. That such a large number of her stories show conflict between generations, who yet maintain their mutual loyalty, only highlights the importance she attaches to family identity, and other forms of intimate relationships, for it is by reacting among intimates, or in a close-knit group, that each individual defines himself, increases his own self-awareness and enlarges his concept of reality.

When her characters suffer from emotional aridity or entropy — as they often do — it more often comes from inhibition, isolation or lack of emotional experience, not from the emotional over-stimulation which Lorenz finds such a common modern condition. Very few of her stories are about the sophisticated. When 'cultured' people appear they are treated ironically, as in 'Miss Holland' or 'A Woman Friend'; while she is even more caustic about those aping the manners of the supposedly cultured, such as the Beckers or Miss Lomas.

Mary Lavin has chosen to remain within a limited artistic field, geographic, sociological and emotional, in order to concentrate on the dramatic representation of feeling. Her narrow scenic field yet magnifies the human heart and creates a microcosm within which reality becomes magnified. She avoids the strong stimuli of sensationalism, in all its forms. She tries to release the reader's capacity to feel by stressing the neglected inner human concerns, arising from simple, sometimes banal, and only occasionally dramatic, situations. These inner realities she reveals as often strangulated by social and religious convention, or various other forms of psychological determinism. 'Things are not what they seem', and 'we must stop reacting to preconceived patterns', are two of her dicta.

A recent story illustrates this. In 'A Mug of Water', the honeymoon couple walking in Mayo go to a cottage for a drink. The woman of the house fills a mug with water, then hesitates and hands it back to a girl who emerges from within. The girl is lithe, beautiful, until she turns her head, and reveals one side of her face ravaged by some accident or disease. Things are not what they seem. Her character's reaction of repulsion is piqued by curiosity tinged with pity. The momentary revelation ends this story to which each reader is left to react in his own way. Mary Lavin always avoids arousal of fascinated disgust, harped upon in so much modern writing.

That we must stop reacting to preconceived patterns is shown in a recent story 'Senility', which the *New Yorker* refused to publish because its subject, delicately treated, is the shame of incontinence. The description of torture is frequent in the press; almost all taboos on sex as a subject have been removed. Why therefore should we shy away from other intimacies of the human body? Evidently Mary Lavin thinks we are curiously inconsistent in this respect.

The old dangers of habitual reaction caused by narrow lives and too much adherence to proscribed patterns of thought, which crop up so frequently in Mary Lavin's early work, may have been largely removed in western society, but the dangers now are to ignore one's roots, have superficial values based on expediency which exclude an understanding of the nature of love, and be so brain-washed by external stimuli that entropy results from glutted, not strangulated, feelings.

Mary Lavin's quiet rebellion is against all those contemporary tendencies which lead to distorted or undeveloped awareness, against which modern thinkers

and critics warn in different ways.[2] This includes the
secularisation of love, using this word in its broadest
sense.[3] She implicitly condemns a society whose
educated people tend to become less, rather than more,
perceptive because they are obsessed with technical
or material progress. She believes modern man is so busy
doing, that he has no time for being. Men are valued too
often only for what they do or have, not for their use-
fulness and effectiveness as persons, and her stories
communicate these views obliquely. She is conscious
of her handicaps and responsibilities as a woman writer.
This is a further reason why she avoids being too
explicit and concentrates on those finer areas of sensibility, to which the feminine element in our natures is
in general more responsive.

What then is Mary Lavin's specific contribution to
literature as a short story writer, for it is as such that she
sees herself. In her 1959 Preface she said:

> I even wish that I could break up the two long novels
> I have published into the few short stories they ought
> to have been in the first place. For in spite of these
> two novels, and in spite of the fact that I may write
> other novels, I feel that it is in the short story that a
> writer distills the essence of his thought. I believe
> this because the short story, shape as well as matter,
> is determined by the writer's own character. Both
> are one . . . . Because of this conviction that in a
> true story, form and matter are one, I cannot attach
> the same importance as the critics to brevity and
> relevance. It is surely significant that the great short
> stories of the world have often been studded with
> irrelevancies. It is to the magical risks that have been
> taken with the short story that we often owe their
> most magical embellishments. It is a question whether

we really want perfection in this medium as much as we are told that we do in the textbooks. Do we? And if we do, how is it that the early stories of Chekhov can give such pleasure, and the unfinished stories of Katherine Mansfield such satisfaction? Much as we rejoice in the universality of art I think art speaks with its fullest voice when the note of particularity is not lost in that of universality, nor time in that of eternity.

The short story genre is necessarily empirical, stylistically plural and eclectic.[4] The judgment on any writer in this genre will be made as a result of the compulsion, or reader-appeal, which arises from imaginative strength in his work. The contemporary reader is also interested in fictional forms which enlarge his comprehension of human motives in a setting to which he can relate. The possible variety within the short story form is legion, but every writer's choice of modes obviously reflects aspects of his historicity. What may appeal to contemporaries may therefore be viewed by and appeal very differently to future generations. Given these contingencies we can see that Mary Lavin tries to introduce a perspective through her writing which releases and reveals what to her is the real spirit of life as she sees it. This is a fuller life, as it may be known once intervening materiality is discarded.

Mary Lavin's work gives further artistic expression to Virginia Woolf's definition:

Life is not a series of gig-lamps symmetrically arranged; life is a luminous halo, a semi-transparent envelope surrounding us from the beginning of consciousness to the end. It is not the task of the novelist to convey this varying, this unknown and uncircumscribed spirit, whatever aberration or complexity it may display, with as little mixture of the alien and external as possible? We are not pleading merely for courage and sincerity; we are suggesting that the proper stuff of fiction is a little other than custom would have us believe it.[5]

In order to convey the texture of reality more closely Mary Lavin generally frees her characters from the linear grip of plot, away from the old form of fictional realism with its chronological sequences reflecting a more stable and contained society. Instead of plot she uses other aesthetic devices such as motifs and symbols. The reliable, omniscient and intrusive narrator of some early stories becomes, as she progresses, the single, more fallible narrator; or she uses multiple viewpoints – all more or less limited. In her later work she shows a complex and fluid handling of time in which memory is important. She includes both the irrational and the subconscious, oblique and random stimuli. Her work is also a commentary on the double meanings and duplicities of modern existence, with its uncertain values. This 'modern' handling of the genre is an inevitable result of the shrinking modern world, in which we know that the definition of reality varies not only from culture to culture, as it does from person to person, but also depends on the particular linguistic vehicle, in this case English. Mary Lavin is a modern writer in her awareness, and in her conveyance, of all these contingencies.[6]

As with the work of James Joyce, Lavin's stories centre round the dominant consciousness of one character, the intermingling of several, or on the communication of consciousness between characters and the author. The discoveries in her stories often concern small psychic growths, or revelations of an awareness, or a lack of it. It is evident therefore that she is more than a provincial Irish writer, though she most often prefers to set her stories in the Irish scene.

Sociological implications of religion, the open discussion of death, the fact that the existence of a transcendental dimension is taken for granted, a certain strain of fantastic humour, all this is specifically, though not exclusively, Irish. Only her few Gaelic background stories could be called Irish in theme and even here their echoes are enduring ones, for her concerns go beyond time and place. Her later work has become increasingly concerned with psycho-socio forces not registered in documentary modes of fiction, such as the modern cruelty of freedom which appears in 'Trastevere'.

Lavin's earlier stories about stable small town life in Ireland, set in the earlier part of this century, should be read in relation to her later work. The past continues to be an important element in her fabulations of reality, so does intuition, instinctual patterns and heightened perceptions. Mary Lavin's use of the past in the short story genre is similar to the way many modern novelists have contrasted the flexible, contingent and disillusioned present day with a stable element from the past by using a mythical archetype, literary model or *alter ego*.[7] By reading a short story writer in this way, taking and comparing stories of different types, one can obtain the same artistic 'depth' as from a sustained piece of writing in a novel.

In as far as Mary Lavin can be 'placed' (an objectionable term) as a short story writer, she belongs to that large group of artists who have written lyric short stories, the spirit of which can be identified with Frank O'Connor's 'lonely voice'. A recent attempt to sketch the development of such stories traces it through Turgenev, Chekhov, Mansfield, S. Anderson, Woolf, Coppard, Welty and Updike, and points out that the lyric short story needs to achieve exact balance between realistic detail and delicate suggestiveness, subordinating outward action to inner feeling.[8] One could, of course, add other names to this list.

It is Turgenev and Chekhov who first moved the story away from reported action, making it possible to tell a story about subtle changes in feeling and emotion, and this is the type Mary Lavin writes. She was early compared by both Lord Dunsany and V. S. Pritchett to the Russian writers, but denies being influenced technically by them. She says that she perhaps owes most to Edith Wharton, Sarah Orne Jewett and George Sand.[9] Nevertheless she admires Chekhov, whom she considers father of the European short story. Her other most admired writers are Joyce, O'Flaherty, Sean Ó Faoláin, Elizabeth Bowen, Katharine Anne Porter and Eudora Welty.

It is evident from the didactic strain present in Mary Lavin's early stories such as 'Brigid', 'Magenta', 'Sarah', 'Brother Boniface', and others that moral idealism is one of her artistic motivating forces. Some of her earlier work makes its message obvious by the over-explicit use of symbolic imagery such as the sheep-raddle in 'Sarah'. Among early stories those in which ironic implication is pronounced, such as 'The Becker Wives', 'A Happy Death', 'At Sallygap', but which keep the message in the background and subordinate the didactic to the dramatic, emerge as artistically superior.

In contemporary Anglo-Irish literature Mary Lavin stands apart in her deliberate restraint, her decision to concentrate on the inner play of feeling to the exclusion of political documentation. A recent reviewer called her 'The Vermeer of the Irish short story'.[10] She is nearest to Joyce in her attempts to enlarge areas of consciousness, but at once more ironic and less allusive, more compassionate and less sardonic; more inhibited and less explicit than he, and her aesthetic base is intuitive rather than philosophical. Her fastidiousness is partly social choice but also perhaps an inability to face up to the depths of her own nature, and to the confusions of modern society with its strong strain of nihilism. She believes that the shape and matter of the short story is determined by the writer's own character and that 'both are one', yet there are further depths which have not as yet been plumbed. It is here, researching into her own inhibitions, that Mary Lavin will continue to contribute to literature.

Apart from the fact that she is still writing, Mary Lavin's contribution to the short story genre will not receive its full acknowledgement until she is more generally understood, and appreciated, as a writer. Her reserved, oblique, sometimes ambiguous implications are demanding. Her work reflects the customary Irish tendency to present multiple and opposing points of view. There are often two ways of interpreting events, and the Irish — they are not alone in this — have always been masters of half-meanings. Is this one reason why Ireland is today producing a high number of competent writers and poets? For this is an age in which the half-meaning is the nearest anyone can get to being categoric.

As Mary Lavin is a writer who stresses the importance of the intuitive, mystical and non-verbal areas of human understanding, I believe the survival values of her work will depend upon a more general appreciation of these aspects. Is it because she comes from a linguistically gifted race with a long tradition of oral literature that the plasticity of an earlier dimension of consciousness, wider and more subtle than that which now pertains in western society, and impossible to produce in words, yet adheres to Mary Lavin's writing? There is in all her work a sense of meaning present to the mind as an unexpressed essence, a distillation of feeling, which demands more than eye-reading. As time goes on one hopes that more and more readers will grasp the significance of this, whether she be read for her social revelation of a particular milieu in Ireland, or for her humane enlargement of reality giving greater scope for mutual human communication.

Notes on the Text

INTRODUCTION

1 Zack Bowen, *Mary Lavin*, Bucknell University Press, Irish Writers Series (Cranbury, New Jersey 1975).

2 More information about Mary Lavin's debut as a writer, and the encouragement she received from Lord Dunsany is to be found in Robert W. Caswell, 'Mary Lavin: Breaking a Pathway', *Dublin Magazine* VI (1967), 32-44. See also Lavin's introduction to *Tales from Bective Bridge*, 1978 edition.

3 Augustine Martin, 'A Skeleton Key to the Stories of Mary Lavin' *Studies* LII, Winter 1963, 393.

4 Frank O'Connor, *A Short History of Irish Literature: a backward look* (New York 1968), 229.

5 V. S. Pritchett's introduction to Mary Lavin's *Collected Stories* (Boston 1971), 2-3.

CHAPTER 1

1 V. S. Pritchett, *Dublin: a portrait* (London 1967), 7 and 30. See also *Midnight Oil* (London 1971), 119-20, volume two of his autobiography.

T. P. Coogan in *Ireland Since the Rising* (London 1966), 177, supports Pritchett's view when he says: '. . . in the 1930s, in the mingled disillusionment and fervour of post Civil War nationalism, the portcullis was lowered on the outside world. Within the citadel, the cultural gaze was turned inward and backward to some supposedly pure and blessed era in Ireland's past . . . . Such influences as did penetrate to reach the rank and file were, ironically, almost exclusively Anglo-Saxon . . . . Popular taste is still basically Edwardo-Georgian with strong residual traces of Victorian forms.'

2 R. D. Laing, *The Politics of Experience and the Bird of Paradise* (London 1967), discusses the reasons behind such behaviour.

3 Zack Bowen, *Mary Lavin* (New Jersey 1975), 23.

4 Frank O'Connor, *The Lonely Voice* (New York 1968), 'The girl at the gaol gate', 396.

5 In such stories Mary Lavin comes up against what Sean Ó Faoláin called 'The Dilemma of Irish Letters'. Writing at the same period when Mary Lavin was composing her earlier work, he points out that the dissolution of the old Anglo-Irish ascendancy, which so obviously frames the social scene, has led to an over-simplifying of the social picture. See *The Month* II No. 6 new series, Dublin 1949, 373, and 375-6.

CHAPTER 2

1 A woman writer, for example, is unlikely to write in these terms: 'Blind, the night has shrunk to the dimensions of the wasted penis — the hollow reed in which life is carried and generated: shrivelled under the taut stars like an empty paint-tube'. Lawrence Durrell, *The Black Book — an agon* (Paris 1938), 100.

2 This passage recalls the *Book of Isaiah*, 'as a sheep before the shearers is dumb, so he openeth not his mouth'. (Chapter 53, v.5).

3 The character of Bedelia, Mary Lavin says owes something to her maternal grandmother who was orphaned aged thirteen, married the shop assistant aged sixteen and became matriarch of a large family.

4 Frank O'Connor, *The Lonely Voice: a study of the short story* (Cleveland and New York 1963), edition used Bantam 1968. Quotes this story as probably Mary Lavin's finest (p.395).

5 This is the same Mad Mary who appears in 'Lemonade' and 'Sunday brings Sunday'.

6 Mary M. Machen, a review of *The Long Ago* stories in *Studies* 33, Sept. 1944, 428.

7 This has already been pointed out by Robert W. Caswell in a perceptive criticism of this story, 'The Human Heart's Vagaries', *Kilkenny Review* 12-13, Spring 1965, 77-8.

8 Mary Lavin's treatment of marriage is noticeably reticent about the effects of alcoholism, unlike most Irish writers. See T. P. Coogan's 'Marriage: till drink us do part!' *The Irish: a personal view* (London 1975).

9 Thomas J. Murray, 'Mary Lavin's World: lovers and strangers', *Eire-Ireland* 7, 1972, 127.

'Although Manny's complacency makes him a sexually impotent husband, it is finally his kindness and softness, too frail to contain the animal lustiness she had once hoped to find in marriage, which she insists on battling as weakness.

The Annie Ryans of Lavin country are legion. Their husbands' small and delicate strengths are never judged or used psychologically on their own terms for what they are. Their vicarious pleasures in other women's sexuality are joyless and illusionary.'

10 Robert W. Caswell, 'Irish Political Reality and Mary Lavin's *Tales from Bective Bridge, Eire-Ireland* 3, Spring 1968, 53-4.

11 See chapter 4 of this study for further consideration of this story.

12 Frank O'Connor, op. cit., 394.

13 T. P. Coogan, *Ireland since the rising,* (London 1966), 178.

14 Frank O'Connor, op. cit., 395.

15 Janet E. Dunleavy, in her article 'The Fiction of Mary Lavin: universal sensibility in a particular milieu', reprinted *Irish University Review,* Autumn 1977, 222-36, asks: 'Are James and Myra unable to withstand the hereditary forces which determine male and female natures, do they succumb in the end to those environmental influences that pressure even those on the fringes of society to accept traditional male and female roles?' (p.232).

CHAPTER 3

1 Brid Mahon, 'The Quiet Authoress', article about Mary Lavin written on the occasion of the conferral of a D.Litt. (Hon.), *Sunday Press* (Dublin) 21 April 1968, 20.

2 'The Saturday Interview, Maev Kennedy talked to Mary Lavin', *The Irish Times,* 13 March 1976, 4.

3 'Maimie Sully' is an example of a character named for the qualities he/she illustrates in the story, a favourite Lavin device. This woman both maims and sullies her husband Elgar.

4 Because her criticism is veiled in irony Mary Lavin was one of the few leading Irish writers whose work was never banned by the Censorship Board. Kate O'Brien's *Land of Spices* (1941), for example, was banned because of a single direct reference to homosexuality.

5   Edna O'Brien, 'An Irish Childhood', *The New Review* II No. 23, 23 Feb. 1976, 27-36. The same opinion appears in *Mother Ireland* (London 1976).

6   Sean Ó Faoláin, 'A Portrait of the Artist as an old man', *Irish University Review*, Spring 1976, 10-18.

7   This story was omitted from *Tales from Bective Bridge* by the publisher without consulting the author and appeared two years later in *The Long Ago*.

8   Sean Ó Faoláin, *The Irish*, revised edition (London 1969), 119.

9   Robert Caswell, 'The Human Heart's Vagaries', *Kilkenny Magazine*, Spring 1965, 69-89. The significance of the names of the three students is discussed in this article.

10   See Philip O'Keefe, 'Knock Shrine. Last of its kind', *Hibernia*, 20 August 1976, 10. He explains that in 1969 it was decided to build something at Knock (population 350) to accommodate pilgrims to the site of an alleged apparition of ninety-seven years before. The original simple plan grew to a huge octagonal church with seating for 7,500 indoors, whose spire can be seen for miles. The church is estimated to have cost over £1 million plus the cost of a new ring road and car parks paid for by the local council. More than half the work was paid for by money largely coming from the United States. A new infirmary for the sick is to be constructed and 750,000 pilgrims are expected annually. The Shrine is dedicated to Our Lady Queen of Ireland. The Pope visited Knock in 1979.

11   Augustine Martin, 'A Skeleton Key to the Stories of Mary Lavin', *Studies* LII, Winter 1963, 404. This article mentions the pervasive presence of death in Lavin stories and says: 'An investigation of its provenance and causes would be unlikely to yield much of critical value — in fact it could be explained better in terms of sociology and Irish sociology in particular'.

12   In early Irish crosses, such as that of Monasterboice (*circa* A.D. 923), the kingship, triumph and glory of the crucifixion is stressed and the crucified figure does not appear; when it does at this period it is robed and resigned, rather than tortured; Christ the Son of God rather than Christ the son of man. An early Athlone crucifix plaque of the eighth century in the National Museum, Dublin, shows such a dignified Christ figure, his cross supported by angels. The realistic, suffering human figure did not become common until later.

13   See A. T. Lucas, 'Penal Crucifixes', *County Louth Archaeological Journal* XIII, 2, 1964 (Dundalk 1955), 145-72. Speaking of the penal crosses Lucas says: 'Remembering the religious and social disabilities of the Catholics of the time they

must have played a very important part in the devotional life of the people. In the absence of the woodcuts, pictures, statues and other religious emblems which discrimination, poverty, and isolation prevented them from acquiring they must have formed the sole focus of family devotions in thousands of homes'.

14 Irish poets reflect this expiatory theme, as in Patrick Pearse's 'The Rebel', with its strong biblical overtones:

> *God the unforgetting, the dear God that loves the peoples*
> *For whom he died naked, suffering shame.*

Plunkett's 'I see his Blood upon the Rose' at least sees the cross as 'every tree' and therefore a symbol of life as well as suffering. Yeats sought outside Christianity for his life-asserting ethic. Poets subsequent to Ireland's independence have continued to put the accent on the 'terrible' rather than the 'beauty' of his famous line 'a terrible beauty is born'.

W. R. Rodgers, a Belfast Presbyterian parson, is one of the few modern Irishmen who has written much on religious subjects. In his 'Resurrection: an Easter sequence', God dies on the cross and is reborn — the end is hopeful.

Rodgers' Catholic counterpart, Padraig de Brun, wrote a magnificent but penitential sequence of poems in Irish entitled 'Miserere'.

15 Teilhard de Chardin, *Le Milieu Divin*, written 1929, (London 1964) 102. 'Far too often the Cross is presented for our adoration, not so much as a sublime end to be attained by our transcending ourselves, but as a symbol of sadness, of limitations and repression'.

16 The horrific, now sanctioned and more likely to impress, is illustrated by the work of Guido Rocha, whose powerful crucifix reproduces his own torture in South American prisons. This was exhibited at the World Council of Churches Assembly, Nairobi 1975. It shows an emaciated and naked figure writhing and shrieking on the cross, the raised knees an apex of pain.

17. See Note 1 above.

CHAPTER 4

1 George Sand, *La Mare au Diable* 1846 (edition used Garnier-Flammarion, Paris 1964), 39.

2 'Bridal Sheets' is touched by that spirit of the grotesque which, combined with fantasy, Vivian Mercier finds to be the two emphases of specifically Irish humour. *The Irish Comic Tradition* (Oxford 1969), 11.

3   'The Great Wave' could be usefully compared with the powerful description of the storm in chapter 16 of Walter Macken's *Rain on the Wind* (London 1950), and Liam O'Flaherty's short story 'The Oar' (first published 1928).

4   'The Mouse' connects with two earlier stories, 'The Convert' and 'Limbo'.

5   Benedict Kiely, *Modern Irish Fiction — a critique* (Golden Eagle Books, Dublin 1950), 58.

6   James Stephens, *The Crock of Gold* (edition used, London 1965), 91-2.

'And all would be well if Thought would but continue to frolic, instead of setting up first as *locum tenens* for Intuition and sticking to the job, and afterwards as the counsel and critic of Omnipotence. Everything has two names and everything is twofold . . . . There has been no matrimony of minds, but only an hermaphroditic propagation of automatic ideas . . . .'

7   George Steiner, *After Babel* (London and New York 1975), 465.

'The words we speak bring with them far more knowledge, a far denser charge of feeling than we consciously possess; they multiply echo. Meaning is a function of social-historical antecedent and shared reponse.'

8   Lawrence Durrell, *An Irish Faustus* (New York 1964).

9   'At Sallygap' is discussed from a different point of view in chapter 2.

10   Whether deliberately or not Mary Lavin reveals the necessity for what a speaker at a recent Symposium on World Spiritualities touched upon: 'A spirituality suited to contemporary man must rest on the drive we feel for a total experience of the real. This is what sends men into the primordial past as well as into the distant future, into the outer dimension of the universe as well as into the fantastic worlds hidden in the smallest particles of matter. We must walk on the moon both as a physical experience and as a mystical symbol of our inner journey into ourselves. This drive towards the real also includes the imperative quest of mankind to understand the deepest realms of the unconscious self as this is indicated by symbols revealed in dreams. Thomas Berry, 'Contemporary Spirituality: the journey of the human community', *Crosscurrents*, XXIV, Summer-Fall 1974, 180.

CHAPTER 5

1   Arthur Koestler, *The Act of Creation* (Hutchinson, London 1969), 334.

2 Two other re-written novels are Malcolm Lowry's auto-biographical first novel, *Ultramarine*, published 1933, revised and reprinted posthumously 1963; and John Fowles' *Magus*, also his first novel, begun in 1950, frequently revised and published 1965, revised again and reprinted 1977. The author's foreword discusses his reasons for revision.

3 From Tennyson's *Maud*, Part I.

'There has fallen a splendid tear
From the passion-flower at the gate'.

4 The most recently revised texts are 'Lilacs', 'Love is for Lovers' and 'Miss Holland' in *Tales from Bective Bridge*, 1978.

CONCLUSION

1 Konrad Lorenz, *Civilised Man's Eight Deadly Sins*, trans. M. Latzke, (Methuen, London 1974). The eight sins are: over-population, devastation of the environment, man's race against himself, entropy of feeling, genetic decay, the break with tradition, indoctrinability, nuclear weapons.

2 Theodore Roszak, *Where the Wasteland Ends, Politics and Transcendence in post industrial society* (New York 1972, edition used Faber, London 1974), 77 says: 'What authentically escapes our awareness, we are free to dismiss as unreal, non-existent. Yet my contention is that the universe of single vision, the orthodox consciousness in which most of us reside most of the time and especially when we are being most 'wide awake' and 'realistic', is very cramped quarters, by no means various and spacious enough to let us grow to full human size.'

3 See Erich Fromm's *The Art of Loving* (edition used Unwin, London 1975).

4 Ian Reid's *The Short Story* (Methuen, London; Barnes & Noble, New York 1977) is a useful discussion of the genre with selective bibliography.

5 Virginia Woolf, *Collected Essays* Vol 2, 'Modern Fiction', (Hogarth, London 1972), 106.

6 P. L. Berger and Th. Luckmann's *The Social Construction of Reality* (Doubleday, New York 1966) discusses to what degree our cognitive functions are influenced by what the culture to which we belong considers to be 'real' and 'true'.

7 There are many recent examples in fiction of this. Both John Fowles and Muriel Spark make use of such devices, so does Francis Stuart in *A Hole in the Head* (London 1977), whose protagonist has visitations from the shade of Emily Brontë,

and Brian Moore whose *The Great Victorian Collection* (New York and London 1975) creates reality from a dream.

    8 Eileen Baldeshwiler, 'The lyric short story: the sketch of a history', *Studies in Short Fiction* VI, Summer 1969, No. 3., 443-54.

    9 *St. Stephen's* (Trinity Term, No. 12, 1967), 22. Quoted by Robert Caswell in 'Irish Political reality and Mary Lavin's *Tales from Bective Bridge*', *Eire-Ireland* 3 (Spring 1968), 48-60.

    10 Tom MacIntyre's 'Review of *The Shrine and Other Stories*', *Books Ireland* 16, Sept. 1977, 171-2.

Bibliography

1. BOOKS (short story collections unless otherwise indicated)

A *Tales from Bective Bridge*, Boston: Little, Brown, 1942; London: Michael Joseph, 1943; Dublin: Poolbeg Press, 1978. (Awarded James Tait Black Memorial Prize)

B *The Long Ago and other stories*, London: Michael Joseph, 1944.

C *The House in Clewe Street* (novel), London: Michael Joseph, 1945; Boston: Little, Brown, 1945. (Serialised under the title of *Gabriel Galloway* in the *Atlantic Monthly*, (November 1944 - May 1945, seven instalments).

D *The Becker Wives*, London: Michael Joseph, 1946; New York: New American Library, 1971.

E *At Sallygap*, Boston: Little, Brown, 1947.

F *Mary O'Grady* (novel), London: Michael Joseph, 1950; Boston: Little, Brown, 1950.

G *A Single Lady and other stories*, London: Michael Joseph, 1951.

H *The Patriot Son and other stories*, London: Michael Joseph, 1956.

I *A Likely Story* (juvenile), New York: Macmillan, 1957; Dublin: Dolmen Press, 1967.

J *Selected Stories*, New York: Macmillan, 1959.

K *The Great Wave and other stories*, London: Macmillan, 1961; New York: Macmillan, 1961. (Awarded Katherine Mansfield Prize).

L   *The Stories of Mary Lavin* (volume I), London: Constable, 1964.
M   *In the Middle of the Fields and other stories*, London: Constable, 1967; New York: Macmillan, 1969.
N   *Happiness and other stories*, London: Constable, 1969; Boston: Houghton Mifflin, 1970.
O   *Collected Stories*, Boston: Houghton Mifflin, 1971.
P   *The Second Best Children in the World* (juvenile), London: Longmans Young Books, 1972; Boston, Houghton Mifflin, 1972.
Q   *A Memory and other stories*, London: Constable, 1972; Boston: Houghton Mifflin, 1973.
R   *The Stories of Mary Lavin* (volume II), London: Constable, 1973.
S   *The Shrine and other stories*, London: Constable, 1977.

FORTHCOMING SELECTIONS:

The Stories of Mary Lavin, Volume III. London: Constable.
Selected short stories, Harmondsworth: Penguin.

2.   POEMS

'Let me come inland always', *Dublin Magazine*, 15 (January-March 1940), 1-2.
'Poem', *Dublin Magazine*, 15 (January-March 1940), 2.

3.   ESSAYS, REVIEWS AND INTERVIEWS

Preface to *Selected Stories*, New York: Macmillan, 1959, pp. v-viii; reprinted in *The Irish Press*, 27 April 1968.
Review of *Some Curious People* by Brinsley MacNamara, *The Bell*, 10 September 1945, 547-49.
'The Quiet Authoress', an interview with Brid Mahon on the occasion of the conferral of a D.Litt. (Hon), *Sunday Press*, Dublin, 21 April 1968, 20.
'The Saturday interview: Maev Kennedy talked to Mary Lavin', *The Irish Times*, March 13 1976, 4.

4. SECONDARY SOURCES ABOUT MARY LAVIN —
   A SELECTION

Bowen, Zack, *Mary Lavin,* The Irish Writers Series, a bio-graphical-critical introduction. Lewisburg: Bucknell University Press and London: Associated University Presses, 1975.

Caswell, Robert W., 'The Human heart's Vagaries', *Kilkenny Review,* 12-13, Spring 1965, 69-89.

Caswell, Robert W., 'Mary Lavin: Breaking a Pathway', *Dublin Magazine,* 6, 1967, 32-44.

Caswell, Robert W., 'Irish Political Reality and Mary Lavin's *Tales from Bective Bridge*', *Eire-Ireland* 3, Spring 1968, 48-60.

Deane, Seamus, book review of *The Stories of Mary Lavin* volume II, *Irish University Review,* Autumn 1974, 283-85.

Driscoll, Joanne, 'Mary Lavin and the Irish Split-Personality', *The Critic* (New York) 22, December 1963-January 1964, 20-23.

Dunleavy, Janet E., 'The Double Vision of Mary Lavin: universal sensibility in a particular milieu', *The Uses of Historical Criticism: Essays in honor of Irving Ribner,* eds. R. H. Canary, C. Huffmann & H. Kuzicki, University of Pittsburgh Press, 1974/5: Reprinted "The Fiction of Mary Lavin: universal sensib: etc. . . .", *Irish University Review,* Autumn 1977, 222-36. 'Men in Mary Lavin's Fiction', *Canadian Journal of Irish Studies,* II, 1, May 1976, 10-14.

Dunsany, Lord, 'A Preface', *Tales from Bective Bridge,* London, Michael Joseph 1943, 5-8.

Garfitt, Roger, 'Constants in Contemporary Irish Fiction', *Two Decades of Irish Writing — A critical Survey,* ed. Douglas Dunn, Cheadle Hulme, Carcanet Press, 1975, 232-4.

Kiely, Benedict, 'Mary Lavin', *Modern Irish Fiction: A Critique,* Dublin, Golden Eagle Books, 1950, 57-8, 92-3.

Martin, Augustine, 'A Skeleton Key to the Stories of Mary Lavin', *Studies* 52, Winter 1963, 393-406.

Murphy, C. A., *Imaginative Vision and Story Art in Three Irish Writers, Sean Ó'Faoláin, Mary Lavin, and Frank O'Connor.* Dissertation, Trinity College, Dublin, 1968.

Murray, Thomas J., 'Mary Lavin's World: Lovers and Strangers', *Eire-Ireland* 7, 1972, 122-31.

O'Connor, Frank, 'The Girl at the Gaol Gate', *A Review of*

English Literature, 1, April 1960, 25-33, rprinted in *The Lonely Voice: a Study of the Short Story,* Cleveland and New York, World 1963, 202-13, Bantam 1968, 389-97.

Peterson, R. F., *Mary Lavin,* New York: Twayne's English Authors Series, 1978.

Pritchett, V. S., 'Introduction', *Collected Stories,* Boston, Houghton Mifflin, 1971, ix-xiii.

Roark, B. J., 'Mary Lavin: the local and universal'. Dissertation, University of Colorado, 1968.

FORTHCOMING

Irish University Review: A Journal of Irish Studies, Volume 9 Number 2 Autumn 1979 is a special issue devoted to Mary Lavin. It includes: Catherine Murphy, 'Mary Lavin: An Interview', and 'Afterword' by Mary Lavin; Janet E. Dunleavy, 'The Making of Mary Lavin's "Happiness" '; Mary Lavin, 'A Family Likeness'; Marianne Koenig, 'Mary Lavin: the Novels and the Stories'; Bonnie Kime Scott, 'Mary Lavin and the Life of the Mind'; Heinz Kosok, 'Mary Lavin: A Bibliography'.

Appendix

Alphabetical List of Short Stories

Short stories published in periodicals and short story collections. The code numbers used are listed under 'books' in the bibliography. Some references to publication in anthologies are included.

SEPARATE PUBLICATION	*Book Code*
'Akoulina of the Irish Midlands, An', *Dublin Magazine*, 30, July-Sept. 1954, 6-19	H, R.
'Assigh', *Cosmopolitan*, 143, Jan. 1960, 80-87.	J. Q.
'At Sallygap', *Atlantic Monthly*, 168, Oct. 1941, 464-76.	A, E, O, R.
'Becker Wives, The',	D. R.
'Bridal Sheets', *The New Yorker*, 35, 31 Oct. 1959, 42-49.	K, R.
'Brigid', *Dublin Magazine*, 19, Jan.-Mar. 1944, 8-15; *Great Irish Short Stories*, ed. Vivian Mercier, New York, Dell paperback, 1964; *Studies in Short Fiction*, 2nd edition, ed. Hughes, New York, Holt, Rinehart & Winston, 1974.	J, O, R.
'Brother Boniface',	A, R.
'Bunch of Grape, The', re-written and abridged version in *Ireland of the Welcomes*, 23, 6, Nov.-Dec. 1974, 13-14.	B, L.

Book code

'Cemetery in the Demesne, The', *Microcosm: an*   B, J, L. O.
    anthology of the short story, eds., Gerstenberger
    & Garber, New York, Chandler, 1969.

'Chamois Gloves',   H, J, L.

'Convert, The', *Atlantic Monthly*, 185, Feb. 1950,   G, L.
    51-61.

'Cuckoo-Spit, The', *The New Yorker*, 40, 3 Oct. 1964,   M, O.
    58-62.

'Cup of tea, A',   B, L.

'Daggle-tail', *Pick of the litter: Betty Cavanna's*   uncollected
    Favourite Dog Stories, London, Westminster
    Press, 1952.

'Dead Soldier, The',   A, L.

'Eterna', *The New Yorker*, 8 March, 1976,   S.
    34-40; *The Irish Press*, 4 Sept. 1976.

'Fable, A', *Dublin Magazine*, 15, Oct.-Dec. 1940, 17-26.   A.

'Frail Vessel', *Cosmopolitan*, 149, Nov. 1960,   H, L, O.
    100-06; *The World of Short Fiction, an inter-*
    national collection, 2nd edition, eds. Gullason
    & Casper, New York, Harper & Row, 1971.

'Gentle Soul, A', *Atlantic Monthly*, 219, May 1967,   G, L.
    80-87.

'Girders, The', *Strand Magazine*, 107, May 1944,   uncollected
    62-67.

'Glimpse of Katey, A', *The Bell*, 15, Nov. 1947,   H.
    40-47; *Georgia Review*, 20, Winter 1966,
    401-07.

'Great Wave, The', *The New Yorker*, 35, 13 June   K, L, O.
    1959, 28-37; *Great Modern European Stories*,
    eds. Angus & Angus, New York, Fawcett, 1967;
    The Short Story: an inductive approach, ed.
    Lavin, New York, Harcourt, Brace & World, 1967;
    Great British Short Stories, eds. Huberman &
    Huberman, New York, Bantam 1968.

'Green grave and the black grave, The', *Atlantic*   A, O, R.
    Monthly, 165, May, 1940, 647-55; *Voyage: an*
    anthology of selected stories, ed. Denys Val
    Baker, London, Sylvan Press, 1945, 29-43.

Book code

'Grief', B.

'Happiness', *Modern Irish Short Stories,* N, O.
  ed. David Marcus, London, Sphere Books, 1972.

'Happy Death, A', D, J, L, O.

'Haymaking, The', B.

'Heart of gold', *The New Yorker,* 40, 27 June M.
  1964, 29-38; *The Best American Short Stories,*
  ed. Foley, New York, Ballantine, 1965.

'House to let, A', *Winter's Tales from Ireland I,*
  ed. Augustine Martin, Dublin, Gill & Macmillan,
  London, Macmillan, 1970. [Story taken from
  Mary O'Grady.] *'Ploughshares III,* 1, 1976, 30-32

'In a café', *The New Yorker,* 35, 13 Feb. 1960, 32-39; K, L.
  Stories from the New Yorker; 1950 to 1960,
  New York, Simon & Schuster, 1960; *Women and
  Fiction,* ed. Cahill. New York. New American
  Library, 1975.

'In the Middle of the Fields', *The New Yorker,* 37, M, O.
  3 June 1961, 32-40.

'Inspector's wife, The', B.

'Joy-ride, The', D.

'Lemonade', K.

'Likely Story, A' I, R.

'Lilacs', A.

'Limbo', *Atlantic Monthly,* 193, June 1954, 59-63; H, L.
  Aquarius No. 5, 1972, 122-27.

'Little Prince, The', H, J, L.

'Living, The', *The New Yorker,* 34, 22 Nov. 1958, K, O, R.
  52-56.

'Long Ago, The', B, O, R.

'Long Holidays, The', B, O, R.

'Lost child, The', N.

'Love is for lovers', *Harper's Bazaar,* 76, Jan. 1942, A.
  55, 96, 98, 102-03.

'Loving Memory', *The New Yorker,* 36, 20 August, K, R.
  1960, 32-38.

Book code

'Lucky pair, The', *The New Yorker*, 38, 28 April,   M.
    1962, 39-46.

'Magenta',   D.

'Memory, A',   Q.

'Miss Holland', *Dublin Magazine*, 14, April-June 1939,   A.
    50-62.

'Mock Auction, The',   M.

'My Molly', *What's New*, 209, Christmas 1958, 14-18.   K, R.

'Mouse, The',   K, O, R.

'Mug of water, The', *Southern Review*, 10, 2 April,   S.
    1974, 412-43.

'My Vocation', *Atlantic Monthly*, 197, June 1956,   H, J, L, O.
    49-53.

'New Gardener, The',   N, O.

'Nun's Mother, The', *Great Irish Short Stories*,   B, E, R.
    ed. Vivian Mercier, New York, Dell, 1964.

'Old Boot, An',   H.

'One evening', *Kenyon Review*, 39, Sept. 1967,   N.
    515-25.

'One summer', *The New Yorker*, 41, 11 Sept. 1965,   M.
    50-58; *The Best American Short Stories: 1966*,
    New York, Ballantine, 1966; *By and about Women*,
    (anthology), ed. Schneiderman, New York,
    Harcourt, Brace, Jovanovich, 1973.

'Pastor of Six Mile Bush, The', *Spectrum*, 5, Spring   G.
    1970, Richmond, Virginia Commonwealth University.

'Patriot Son, The', *Georgia Review*, 20, Fall 1966, 301-17. H, L.

'Posy',   G, J, L.

'Pure Accident, A',   N.

'Rabbit, The', *American Mercury*, 57, Nov. 1943,   uncollected
    564-71.

'Sand Castle, The', *Yale Review* NS, 33, June   G, L, O.
    1944, 721-32.

'Sarah',   A, R.

'Say could that lad be I?', *Dublin Magazine*, 16,   A, R.
    July-Sept. 1941, 23-32.

	Book code
'Scylla and Charybdis'.	H.
'Second-Hand', *The New Yorker*, 35, 18 April 1959, 40-48.	K.
'Senility',	S.
'Shrine, The', *Sewanee Review* 82, Spring 1974, 212-46.	S.
'Single Lady, A',	G, L.
'Small bequest, The', *Good Housekeeping*, 118, June 1944, 32-43.	G, J, O, R.
'Story with a pattern, A', *The Bell*, 12, No. 5 Aug. 1946, 220.	G.
'Sunday brings Sunday'	B, O, R.
'Tom', *The New Yorker* 48, Jan. 20, 1973, 34-42; *The Best American Short Stories: 1974*, ed. Foley, Boston, Houghton, Mifflin.	S.
'Tomb of an ancestor',	Q.
'Tragedy, A',	H, L, O.
'Trastevere', *The New Yorker*, 47, 11 Dec. 1971, 43-51.	Q.
'Villas, The', (also published as 'What's wrong with Aubretia'), *Pick of Today's Short stories No. 10*, ed. J. Pudney, London, Putnam, 1959, pp.131-41.	K.
'Villa Violetta',	Q.
'Visit to the cemetery, A',	G, L, O.
'Wet Day, A', *Kenyon Review*, 6, Winter 1944, 10-23.	B, J, R.
'What's wrong with aubretia?' (see 'The Villas')	K.
'Will, The', reprinted in *The Lonely Voice: a study of the short story*, Frank O'Connor, Cleveland and New York, World 1963.	B, J, L.
'Woman Friend, A', *Atlantic Monthly*, 190, July 1952, 43-49.	G, J, R.
'Yellow Beret, The', *The New Yorker*, 36, 12 Nov. 1960, 46-52.	K, R.
'Young Girls, The',	B, L, O.

Index

'Akoulina of the Irish Midlands', 28, 88-9, 130, 155
Anderson, Sherwood, 175
'Asigh', 61, 76
'At Sallygap', 47, 73-5, 115, 122, 123, 132-4, 135, 156-9, 176

Baldeshwiler, Eileen, 185 fn 8
Becker Wives, The, 27
'Becker Wives, The, 19-24, 26, 32, 42, 43-4, 57, 121, 123, 176
Berger, P. L. & Th. Luckmann, 185 fn 6
Berry, Thomas, 184 fn 10
Booth, Wayne C., 112
Bowen, Elizabeth, 176
Bowen, Zack, 26-7, 179 fn 1
'Bridal Sheets', 108, 121-2
'Brigid', 176
'Brother Boniface', 123, 127, 135, 146-7, 155, 176
'Bunch of Grape, The', 145

Caswell, Robert W., 180 fn 7, 181 fn 10, 182 fn 9, 185 fn 9
'Cemetery in the demesne, The', 108
'Chamois gloves', 92, 95-6, 145
Chekhov, Anton, 173, 175, 176
Clarke, Austin, 110
'Convert, The', 87-8
Coogan, T. P., 80, 179 fn 1, 180 fn 8
Coppard, A. E., 175
'Cuckoo-spit, The', 13, 62, 66-8, 128, 129
'Cup of tea, A', 28, 127

'Dead Soldier, The', 108
de Brun, Padraig, 183 fn 14
Dunleavy, Janet E., 181 fn 15
Dunsany, Lord, 10, 176
Durrell, Lawrence, 131, 180 fn 1, 184 fn 8

'Eterna', 50, 96-7, 136

'Fable, A', 145
Fowles, John 184 fn 2, 185 fn 7
'Frail Vessel', 53
Fromm, Eric, 185 fn 3

'Gentle Soul, A', 37-8, 130
'Glimpse of Katey, A', 127
Great Wave, The, 10, 123
'Great Wave, The', 48, 123-4, 130
'Green Grave and the Black Grave, The', 48, 108, 115, 119-21,
    123, 130, 140-41

Happiness, 11
'Happiness', 70-1, 101, 105, 131, 137
'Happy Death, A', 32-6, 42, 43-4, 73, 108, 123, 176
'Haymaking, The', 52-3, 76, 130
'Heart of Gold', 62, 66, 128-9
House in Clewe Street, The, 11, 39, 58

'In a café', 11, 62-5, 67, 122
'Inspector's Wife, The', 51-2, 123
In the Middle of the Fields, 66
'In the Middle of the Fields', 62, 65-6, 130

Jewett, Sarah Orne, 176
Joyce, James, 73, 90, 115, 132, 154, 174, 176
'Joy-ride, The', 27

Kennedy, Maev, 188 fn 2
Kiely, Benedict, 126, 183 fn 5
Koestler, Arthur, 153-4, 184 fn 1

Laing, R. D. 179 fn 1

Lavin, Mary, poems 9-10, 14-15
          critical writing, biographical and autobiographical
          references, 10-11, 85-6, 131, 139, 172-3
'Lemonade', 11, 122, 145
'Likely Story, A', 126-7, 130
'Lilacs', 29-30, 115, 127, 128, 129
'Limbo', 86-7
'Little Prince, The', 53, 54-6
'Living, The', 108, 124, 126
Long Ago, The, 49
'Long Ago, The', 50-1, 135, 148-51, 155
'Long Holidays, The', 142-3
Lorenz, Konrad, 169, 185 fn 1
'Lost Child, The', 101, 106-8, 129, 135
'Love is for Lovers', 72-3, 79, 115, 123, 129
'Loving Memory', 53, 56-8, 79, 108, 124
Lowry, Malcolm, 184 fn 2

Machen, Mary, M. 180 fn 6
MacIntyre, Tom 185 fn 10
Macken, Walter, 183 fn 3
'Magenta', 27, 176
Mahon, Brid, 181 fns 1 & 17
Mansfield, Katherine, 173, 175
Martin, Augustine, 14, 182 fn 11
Mary O'Grady, 11, 70
'Memory, A', 76, 79-82, 128
Mercier, Vivian, 183 fn 2
'Miss Holland', 9, 24-6, 63, 123, 126, 170
'Mock Auction, The', 28, 41-3, 128, 129
Moore, Brian, 185 fn 7
'Mouse, The', 61, 108, 124
'Mug of Water, A', 171
Murray, Thomas J., 180 fn 9
'My Molly', 72, 124-6
'My Vocation', 13, 92, 96, 124

'Nun's Mother, The', 50, 92-5, 127, 159, 163-8

O'Brien, Edna, 48, 76, 90-1, 181 fn 5
O'Brien, Kate, 181 fn 4

O'Casey, Sean 73
O'Connor, Frank, 14, 31-2, 75-6, 175, 179 fn 1, 180 fn 4, 181 fn 14
Ó'Faoláin, Sean, 13, 14, 91, 98-9, 176, 179 fn 1, 181 fn 6 & 8
O'Flaherty, Liam, 14, 176, 183 fn 3
O'Keefe, Philip, 182 fn 10
'Old Boot, An', 53
'One Evening', 135-6
'One Summer', 59-61, 66, 79, 130

'Pastor of Six Mile Bush, The', 99-101, 129
Patriot Son, The, 142
'Patriot Son, The', 122
Pearse, Patrick, 182 fn 14
Plunkett, Joseph, 183 fn 14
Porter, Katharine Anne, 176
'Posy', 27, 38-9, 44, 47, 145
Pritchett, V. S., 14, 17, 22, 176, 179 fn 1
'Pure Accident, A', 76, 101-3

'Rabbit, The', 145
Reid, Ian, 185 fn 4
Rocha, Guido 183 fn 16
Rodgers, W. R., 183 fn 14
Roszak, Theodore, 185 fn 2

'Sandcastle, The', 145
Sand, George, 119, 176, 183 fn 1
'Sarah', 89, 143-4, 176
'Say Could that Lad be I?' 124, 151-3
'Scylla and Charybdis', 28
Second-Best Children of the World, The, 127
Selected Stories, preface to, 11
'Senility', 171
'Shrine, The', 76, 103-5, 110, 135
Single Lady, A, 37
'Single Lady, A', 28-9, 145
'Small Bequest, The', 28, 36-7, 41, 124, 130, 141
Spark, Muriel, 185 fn 7
Steiner, George, 184 fn 7
Stephens, James, 127, 132, 183 fn 6
Stories of Mary Lavin, The, Vol. I, 29

Stories of Mary Lavin, The, Vol. II, 77
'Story with a Pattern, A', 11, 115-17, 124
Stuart, Francis, 185 fn 7
'Sunday brings Sunday', 27, 48-9, 89-108, 123, 148

Tales from Bective Bridge, 10, 115
Teilhard de Chardin, Pierre, 110, 183 fn 15
'Tom', 11, 124, 129, 137
'Trastevere', 11, 69, 72, 175
Turgenev, Ivan, 155, 175, 176

Updike, John 175

'Villa Violetta', 11, 70, 105, 118
'Villas, The', (also entitled 'What's Wrong with Aubretia?'), 39-41,
    45, 59, 76
'Visit to the cemetery, A', 53, 58, 123

Welty, Eudora, 175, 176
'Wet Day, A', 101, 141
Wharton, Edith, 176
'What's Wrong with Aubretia?' (see 'The Villas')
'Widow's Son, The', 115, 118-9
'Will, The', 30-1, 44, 54, 108, 127, 129
'Woman Friend, A', 76, 77-9, 82, 123, 159, 161-3, 170
Woolf, Virginia, 9, 144, 173, 175, 185 fn 5

Yeats, W. B., 183 fn 14
'Yellow Beret, The', 124
'Young Girls, The', 49-50, 127, 159-61